THE BEST OF BREAKFASTS

Also by Joanna Toye

Dangerfield
Shula's Story

THE BEST OF BREAKFASTS

taken from BBC Radio 4's
'On Your Farm'

COMPILED BY JOANNA TOYE

MICHAEL JOSEPH

LONDON

MICHAEL JOSEPH LTD

Published by the Penguin Group
27 Wrights Lane, London W8 5TZ
Viking Penguin Inc., 375 Hudson Street, New York, New York 10014, USA
Penguin Books Australia Ltd, Ringwood, Victoria, Australia
Penguin Books Canada Ltd, 10 Alcorn Avenue, Toronto, Ontario, Canada M4V 3B2
Penguin Books (NZ) Ltd, 182–190 Wairau Road, Auckland 10, New Zealand

Penguin Books Ltd, Registered Offices: Harmondsworth, Middlesex, England

First published in Great Britain 1997
10 9 8 7 6 5 4 3 2 1

Compilation copyright © Joanna Toye, 1997
Illustrations copyright © Zedcor, Inc., 1997
Illustration on page 95 © Julian Cole, 1997
This book is based on the BBC Radio 4 Programme 'On Your Farm'

Set in 10.75/13pt Monotype Ehrhardt
Designed in Quark Xpress on an Apple Macintosh
Printed in England by Clays Ltd, St Ives plc

A CIP catalogue record for this book is available from the British Library

ISBN 0 7181 4231 4

Contents

CONTENTS

To all our breakfast hosts over the years, with thanks.

Preface

The Great British Breakfast is an institution that, in most of Britain, has been in a slow decline for a number of years. But tune in to BBC Radio 4's 'On Your Farm' on Sunday mornings and the listener will discover that the GBB is alive and well, and appearing in all sorts of guises – from scrambled eggs with venison or smoked eel to lavender marmalade, from sourdough bread to potted hough.

For four and a half years I had what was often described as one of the best jobs in the BBC, producing 'On Your Farm'. During that time I had the enviable task of travelling to all corners of rural Britain, visiting places that otherwise I might have passed without a second glance, and sharing breakfast with some fascinating, friendly and welcoming people – all in the name of a radio programme. Not once during those four and a half years were we made to feel anything other than welcome, which is no small order for people unaccustomed to the paraphernalia of broadcasting – having to cope with microphones, trailing leads and grumpy sound engineers; cooking eggs, bacon, mushrooms and toast at the same time as answering the telephone and nursing sick lambs – and finally wondering what questions will be fired at them over the breakfast table.

This book is a tribute to all those people who have taken part, and presents a chance for the programme's incredibly loyal audience to share the recipes with which they have been tempted for so many years.

Time after time, listeners have written saying that the vivid descriptions of the breakfasts have them drooling as they listen to their radios. Now they too can share the secrets of some of Britain's best breakfasts.

I am delighted that Joanna Toye has written this book as, over the last two years, she too has shared the delights, warm welcomes and expanding waistlines of the 'On Your Farm' team. I am sure her book will encourage people to take the trouble to find and then use good local ingredients which, in turn, will help keep the Great British Breakfast alive and well into the twenty-first century.

CAROL TREWIN
Executive Producer (Radio),
Rural Affairs, BBC Birmingham

Compiler's Notes

The idea for this book first surfaced some years ago but, like the best of the breakfasts it describes, it was thoroughly chewed over and digested before I began to draw up lists of possible contributors. I began telephoning round requesting recipes at the beginning of last summer. The responses I got were uniformly enthusiastic and encouragingly authentic. 'Can you hang on a moment, I'm up to my elbows in flour,' said Carla Carlisle. Anne Petch was 'out with the pigs', Jennie Makepeace 'working in the garden'. Nichola Fletcher was keen but pleaded for time: she was off to do a game cookery demonstration at the Royal Highland Show.

Gradually, over the weeks, the recipes began to arrive in the Farming Office in Birmingham. A harassed 'Farming Today' producer, standing by the fax machine in anticipation of details about the latest development in the BSE crisis, was perplexed by the arrival of a recipe for coffee cornflake ice cream. The resident Producer of 'On Your Farm', Alasdair Cross, was called upon to make the ultimate sacrifice – a drawer of his desk to keep the recipes in. Regular presenters Quentin Seddon and Oliver Walston scanned diary and personal organiser respectively in search of those contributors whose breakfasts remained in the memory but whose telephone numbers had vanished into the ether.

This resulting collection has all the charm and individuality of the contributors themselves, the places where they live and work, the variety of foods they produce. For listeners to 'On Your Farm', I hope it will evoke programmes they have enjoyed: for the non-listener I hope it will give a new shape to Sundays and that they will join the million existing listeners at 7.15 on a Sunday morning on Radio Four.

JOANNA TOYE, May 1997

Leo and Sarah Barclay

Kinloch Rannoch, Perthshire

When Leo and Sarah Barclay started selling smoked venison from their farm at Kinloch Rannoch, the most common response was: 'What on earth is it?' In those days, venison itself was a novelty, let alone the idea of smoking it. The Barclays would not have had the idea themselves had not necessity been the mother of invention. Their desire to 'add value' to the output of a typical Scottish hill farm and their need to cull the herd of wild red deer which roamed the farm led to a larder full of haunches of venison. Then came heavy falls of snow which cut them off for weeks: a method of preservation had to be found.

Sarah's first experiments were not in smoking but in salting the meat (in a bath of brine – literally): it was Leo's idea to build a smokery. The approach is, they enthuse, perfect for venison because it tenderises the meat – which is more important with wild venison which can be killed at any age as opposed to farmed venison which is killed at around two years of age. As well as the rich, subtle taste, the resulting product is also a distinctive deep mahogany-red which looks as well as tastes superb in a variety of recipes.

Sarah is a passionate supporter of Scottish foods although she is the first to appreciate the irony of their being cooked by an Englishwoman. Both she and Leo were brought up to love good food and have passed the same appreciation on to their children. The more she has become involved in food production, she says, the more she has realised the amount of good, natural food there is around – created, of course, by an increasing demand from a better-travelled, more discriminating public. What she modestly fails to add is that she and Leo must take much of the credit for creating a market in and an appetite for one such product – smoked venison.

Scrambled Eggs with Smoked Venison

30 g (1 oz) butter
2 really fresh eggs and 1 dessertspoonful of milk
    per person
smoked venison

Melt the butter in a heavy-based pan and add the eggs which you have lightly beaten and seasoned. Stir over a low heat until starting to firm. Add snipped smoked venison at the last minute. Pile onto hot, buttered toast, or serve with:

Oatcakes

This is the traditional Scottish recipe used by the Barclays. The quantity makes 8–10 oatcakes, depending on size.

120 g (4 oz) medium oatmeal
2 tablespoons melted lard
½ teaspoon salt
½ teaspoon baking soda
enough hot water to mix to a stiff dough

Mix all ingredients together and add enough hot water to make a stiff dough. Roll it out to about ¼-inch thick. Cut to desired shape (triangles are traditional) and cook on a hot griddle/frying pan (the hot plate of an Aga or Rayburn is ideal) and cook briefly on both sides. Finally, place on a tray and put in a moderate oven (or the oven of the Rayburn with door open) for 2–3 minutes until crisp and brown. Serve immediately, or cool completely and store in an airtight tin.

Extra – not strictly breakfast recipes
Smoked venison has hundreds of culinary uses. It is a delicious starter, sliced thinly and served with melon or any tropical fruit. Its pungent flavour goes exceptionally well with horseradish cream and a robust salad of rocket leaves. It makes the perfect cocktail party canapé wrapped around prunes, grapes or melon balls, or served on biscuits, wholemeal bread or *ciabatta*. And best of all, for anyone who fears they might blanch at the price of venison steaks, the Barclays sell 300 gram (10 oz) bags of smoked venison offcuts which make a divine pâté.

Smoked Venison and Asparagus Pâté
Serves 10–12 – it is very rich

> 1 tin asparagus bits (not necessarily spears),
>   drained
> 7 oz (200 g) Philadelphia cream cheese
> 10 oz (300 g) smoked venison offcuts
> screw of black pepper
> juice of half a lemon

Place all ingredients in a food processor or liquidiser and blend. This will produce quite a loose mixture. Pile into a bowl and chill. Serve with thin toast, *crudités* or crusty bread, depending on the occasion.

Jayne and Sandy Boyd

Chatsworth, Derbyshire

If Sandy Boyd had to encapsulate his food philosophy in one sentence it would probably be to keep good food well away from accountants. Before taking over the Farm Shop at Chatsworth House, he had worked extensively in the food industry and had become aware of some horrible adulterations in the name of profit: air added to ice cream, and water to bacon – both of which may improve the balance sheet but do little to enhance the taste.

In trying to appeal to a mass market, Sandy thinks that food producers play safe, appealing to the lowest common denominator. And he goes further, describing a scenario with an inverted, but devastating, logic. Nuances of flavour and strength of character are, he asserts, marketed out of food to produce a bland product deemed to be universally acceptable but in fact acceptable to no one. In the driving down of prices and therefore, usually, quality, small specialist producers and retailers can be forced out of business. Large producers then justify their actions by saying there is no market for specialist products – a vicious circle with the small specialist the loser.

Not liking what he was seeing, Sandy began a one-man campaign to reverse the trend. His own experience at companies like Holland and Barratt, Loseley, and Safeway (he is the man who brought muesli to the nation having been responsible for introducing health foods into Safeway stores) was the perfect apprenticeship for Chatsworth. His brief here was to source the shop from the Estate's own farms, introduce more 'added value' products, notably Her Grace's marmalade, jams and lemon curd (very popular in Japan) and, beyond that, to look for supplies from the Estate's tenant farmers and the neighbouring Peak District National Park. Close ties between the retailer and the producer mean that seasonal produce features strongly and the strong regional bias means that the farm shop genuinely reflects its location.

Sandy likens his commitment to regional food to the French concept of *terroir*: the way that the soil and the climate lend a different flavour to the product. Never forget, he admonishes, that food is from the land. It should taste that way.

Sandy and his wife Jayne served a traditional cooked breakfast accompanied by Derbyshire oatcakes. These are thinner and more pliable than a Scottish oatcake and are cooked quickly in the breakfast frying pan once the eggs and bacon have been removed to keep warm.

Derbyshire Oatcakes
Makes 12

270 g (9 oz) medium oatmeal
150 g (5 oz) plain white flour
1 teaspoon salt
15 g (½ oz) fresh yeast
900 ml (1½ pints) warm milk and water, combined

Mix together oatmeal, flour and salt. Dissolve yeast in warm milk and water. Whisk dry ingredients into liquid to make a batter. Cover with a cloth and leave in a warm place for 1 hour. Bake on a greased griddle or in a heavy-based frying pan for 1½ minutes each side. Serve with bacon and eggs, or with butter and jam or cheese.

Helen Browning

Bishopstone, Wiltshire

The Browning family has managed the 1,337 acres of Eastbrook Farm, which is owned by the Church Commissioners, since 1950 but it was only when Helen took over management of the farm from her father in 1986 that she began the conversion to organic systems. Eastbrook Farm and its company Eastbrook Farm Organic Meats have since then become the embodiment of her belief that organic farming is the most appropriate way in which we can continue to feed ourselves healthily.

When Helen walks the fields, she wants to be able to feel as well as see that they are in good heart. She can also hear that they are for the fields are alive with birds – birds, such as the skylark and the Montagu's harrier, which have all but disappeared under conventional systems. The birds are attracted by the insect life, itself an indicator of thriving and varied plant life, as opposed to the sterility of monoculture.

Helen has serious aims and ambitions for Eastbrook but a terrific sense of humour cuts through any intensity. Asked to think about her favourite breakfast after what her marketing manager let slip was 'a bit of a heavy night', she fantasised for a while about Buck's Fizz (made with organic Champagne) before settling, sensibly, if a little queasily, for scrambled eggs, organic bacon, Eastbrook Farm's own smoked breakfast sausages, fresh field mushrooms and 'gallons of coffee'.

General note about sausages (see also *page 23*)

The important thing about sausages is that you do not want to be bothered making small quantities and if you are reliant on a butcher to stuff hog casings for you, he will *certainly* not want to be bothered with small quantities. In a recipe where not much is added in the way of filler (as below), the yield will be just over 5 kg (10 lb) sausages; where a filler like oatmeal or rusk is added, the result will be 5.5 kg (11 lb) sausages from a basic 5 kg (10 lb) meat.

In terms of numbers, the commercial norm issixteen/eight sausages to the kilogram/pound – i.e. eighty sausages will be made from the quantities given in the following recipe. Bearing in mind the domestic cook, the mixture below will work for less provided *all* the quantities are scaled down in proportion – but every recommendation is to bite the bullet and go for the bulk quantity.

Eastbrook Farm's Lamb, Lemon and Apricot Sausages
Makes 5 kg (10 lb) sausages

> 5 kg (10 lb) lamb: two-thirds of which should be
>   breast of lamb, one-third the leaner shoulder
>   meat
> 3 whole organic lemons, roughly zested, quartered,
>   de-pipped
> 480 g (1 lb) soaked dried apricots (or fresh
>   unstoned weight)
> 5 tablespoons lemon juice
> 200 g (7 oz) salt/pepper/ground mace, mixed
>   handful of rusk

Simply place all ingredients (including quartered lemons with pith) into a mincer or food processor and process. Fill into natural sausage casings* and tie off. Exceptionally delicious.

See other sausage recipes for advice about sausage casings or alternative methods, pages 21–2.

Dougal Campbell

Lampeter, Ceredigion

When Dougal Campbell came across some organic pink grapefruit he knew exactly what he wanted to do with them. The resulting jewel-coloured marmalade, containing, as Oliver Walston put it, 'Lego-sized' chunks of peel, was spread thickly on fresh organic brown bread and followed by Dougal's own farmhouse cheeses when 'On Your Farm' breakfasted with him at his home, Tyn Gryg – the House in the Heather – near Lampeter.

During the programme it emerged that, one way and another, Dougal was truly a man of the mountains. A trek to India, where he did some climbing, was followed by time in Switzerland and it was here that he found his vocation. Working first as a fruit and vegetable picker and later as a village *fromagier* in the *alpages* or mountain pastures, he was inculcated in the production of the Gruyère-type cheese, *raclette*.

Returning to the UK, he saw Tyn Gryg for the first time on a rainy March day in 1976. The cottage was little more than a pile of stones but the price of

£14,500 for 46 acres was attractive, as was the solitude. As he milked his four cows day in day out, month in month out, it dawned on him that it was the quality of the grass – and the way in which it was grown – which determined the quality of the milk. Dougal learned by experience the principles of organic farming and, in time, became the producer of Tyn Gryg cheese, a Cheddar-type made on the farm, and Pencarrig, a soft cheese with a white rind and a creamy centre.

Two years after his appearance on 'On Your Farm', and just when things had begun to come good for him, Dougal Campbell was killed, tragically young, in a farm accident in August 1995. However, production of the two cheeses continues at the farm under the supervision of his partner, Marilyn Jones, and the vibrant colour and flavour of his marmalade are a reminder of a man who was full of life.

Dougal Campbell's Marmalade

Dougal asserted that the secret of his marmalade was twofold: firstly the fact that the pink grapefruit was organic, and secondly, the way he wielded the knife. If organic grapefruit are not available, however, the same recipe works well with almost any combination of citrus fruit, e.g. Seville oranges or a mixture of oranges and lemons.

Ingredients – Dougal didn't believe in doing things by halves!

7 kg (14 lb) grapefruit
5 kg (10 lb) granulated sugar

Method – in Dougal's own words:

Chop up the grapefruit coarsely, de-pipping as you go and put the flesh and peel in a huge pan. Add the sugar, heat gently and leave to cook over a low heat on the stove (a Rayburn is ideal) whilst you go for a walk/do the milking. On your return (it will not have boiled all over the stove unless you left the heat too high), spend a restful few minutes or more watching it bubble, stirring from time to time. Then try the drip test: stick in a spoon and watch the way the marmalade drips off the back. It should be neither too drippy nor too globby, but the correct consistency which will permit you to spread it a ¼-inch thick on good fresh organic bread. Then pot it in clean jars with a good airtight seal. Purists say marmalade should be kept but this marmalade can be eaten straight away – although it will keep for up to two years should you have the willpower!

Kenneth and Carla Carlisle

Near Bury St Edmunds, Suffolk

Carla Carlisle has made an extraordinary and enviable culinary journey from America's Deep South toSuffolk, via California, Paris and Burgundy. Every stop on the way is reflected in the menu of the reputed Leaping Hare Café, the restaurant she runs near their Wyken Vineyard near Bury St Edmunds which she persuaded her husband to plant on the perfect, south-facing slopes which had formerly given grudging yields of barley and sugar beet.

When they decided to open the Leaping Hare it was with an antipathy to anything mediocre and a shared fear and loathing of the 'teas and crafts in the barn' syndrome, a feature of so many of the half-hearted farm diversifications of the 1980s. The restaurant/café has gone from strength to strength. That the current cook is Lucy Crabb, formerly of Bibendum in

London is an indication of the standards it aims for and achieves.

Carla describes cooking as 'her passion and her refuge'. Brought up in the Mississipi Delta on the inevitable fried green tomatoes and corn bread, her first experiment in cookery was Louisiana pecan pralines. An encounter with Julia Child's *The Art of Modern French Cooking* at college in New York changed all that and she later took herself (and her already formidable *beurre blanc*) off to France. An *atelier* in Montparnasse was perfect for scanning restaurant menus and inhaling the smell of freshly-baked bread and properly reduced *court bouillon* but the desire to *grow* something led her to Burgundy where she serveda willing apprenticeship to the grapes, the soil, the climate – and the wine maker.

Returning to London, she met her husband – fittingly, at a dinner party. He confessed from the start that wine didn't really interest him. Fortunately, food did – and does.

Despite her world of experience, for her 'On Your Farm' breakfast – in fact, a sumptuous brunch – Carla returned to her muddy Mississipi roots with a triumphant table of the very best of native American cookery.

Pan-fried Quail

In Carla's opinion, quail are 'delicious little birds'. When she was growing up, she says, her family ate them only during the hunting season 'in the fall'. They are now available as farmed birds all year round. Although the flavour is not quite the same, the advantage is that they are not as rare or expensive. For the English palate, Carla adds, she has served this same meal, grits and all, using partridges which are plentiful in Suffolk.

For 6 people: at least 9 quail
  60 g (2 oz) unsalted butter
  4 tablespoons olive oil
  120 g (4 oz) plain flour
  salt and pepper

Butterfly the quail by splitting each bird along the breast bone. Strike with a cleaver to completely flatten. In a small saucepan, melt the butter over a low heat. Allow the solids to settle, then pour off the clarified butter.

Use two large frying pans and heat half the clarified butter and oil in each. Put the flour into a plastic carrier bag (without holes!), add salt and pepper (good, freshly-ground black pepper) and put in the quail, bird by bird, shaking until lightly covered.

Brown the quail on both sides, pressing down as you do. Turn frequently. Reduce the heat, cover the pans loosely, and cook until tender – 15–20 minutes, depending on size.

It is best to serve the birds immediately, but you can keep them warm until serving. Excellent with the grits.

Grits

Anyone who wasn't born and raised in the Deep South tends to think of grits as at best a puzzle and at worst a joke. In fact, they are corn kernels ground coarsely. Made properly, which means nice and creamy, they are delicious. Carla has strong views on grits. 'If you eat lukewarm, dry and lumpy grits, you'll develop a prejudice that will be hard to shake. Do not use Instant Grits which are too bland. Grits should be the last thing you make before sitting down to eat.'

180 g (6 oz) quick grits (grits = polenta or corn-meal)
1½ teaspoons salt
1.5 litres (2½ pints) boiling water
melted unsalted butter

Stir grits slowly into salted boiling water. Return to a slow boil and reduce heat. Cook five minutes, stirring constantly. Top with melted butter when served.

Drop Buttermilk Biscuits
Makes about 18 biscuits

This is the easiest of biscuit recipes because it doesn't require rolling out and cutting. After the butter is cut in, the mixture needs only a few quick strokes before it is ready to drop onto a baking sheet.

240 g (8 oz) plain flour
1 teaspoon salt
2 teaspoons baking powder
½ teaspoon baking soda
100 g (3½ oz) chilled unsalted butter
360 ml (12 fl oz) buttermilk

Pre-heat to the oven to 190°C/375°F/Gas Mark 5.

Sift together the flour, salt, baking powder and baking soda. Add the butter, cut into 6 pieces and blend together with two forks until you have crumbs the size of frozen peas. Add the buttermilk all at once and stir just enough to mix.

Drop by the tablespoon onto ungreased baking sheets. Bake for 12 to 15 minutes, until golden brown. Serve hot.

Refrigerator Strawberry Jam

Carla makes this easy jam – wonderful with the biscuits – when there is a glut of strawberries in the kitchen garden. It tastes, she says, much fresher and nicer than jam made in the normal way and, tightly covered, will keep in the fridge for a long time.

    480 g (1 lb) strawberries
    120 g (4 oz) granulated sugar
    1 teaspoon lemon juice

Wash, hull and quarter the strawberries. In a small stainless or enamel pot stir the fruit and sugar together. Bring to a boil, stir from time to time and then turn the heat down. Add lemon juice and simmer for 8 to 10 minutes, stirring often.

With a slotted spoon remove the fruit and put it in a sterilised jar. Continue simmering the juice until it is reduced by half. Pour it over the fruit. Allow to cool then cover and store in the fridge.

Fig Conserve

Carla remembers the fig tree in her grandmother's backyard groaning with figs every summer. 'We loved them fresh with cream for breakfast', she recalls, 'and in the winter we relived those summer mornings with this fig conserve.'

1 lemon
480 g (1 lb) small ripe figs, trimmed
240 g (8 oz) granulated sugar
60 g (2 oz) chopped pecans

Cut the lemon into quarters and remove seeds. Chop coarsely in a food processor. Put the lemon and figs in a saucepan, add the sugar and boil until thick. Stir in the pecans and then allow to cool. You can either put this into sterilised jars and seal, or refrigerate, covered tightly. Carla stores hers in the fridge and reports that it keeps 'just fine'.

Nick and Sheila Charrington

Layer Marney, Essex

To visit Layer Marney Tower is to step back in time: via the farming methods of the 1930s, through the favoured breeds of the Victorian era, all the way back to the Tudor court in the design and building of the Tower itself. The tallest Tudor gatehouse in the country, it is now surrounded by deer, Dexter cattle and Saddleback pigs which graze freely in the fields in the style of a nineteenth-century naive painting. That Layer Marney is beautiful should be no surprise, given that Nick and Sheila met whilst studying for History of Art degrees. That it is the base for a profitable farming and tourism venture is no surprise either, given the Charringtons' verve and determination.

To their regret, they are not organic – the soil has received so many chemicals over the years that cleansing it is simply not viable within an economic timescale – but they use no growth promoters or antibiotics on their animals. Both the deer and the pigs do well on grass with the minimum of concentrates which are all based on vegetable proteins, and although the Saddleback pigs take roughly twice as long to get to killing weight as a modern commercial breed, the time and their natural diet is reflected in the taste of the meat. The time factor and the expense of feeding a rare-breed animal is the most commonly stated reason for their decline in popularity: the Charringtons are doing their bit to reverse the trend and are producing the most delicious meat into the bargain.

When they began producing venison in 1991, it was still a comparative rarity. Selecting London restaurants at random on the basis that they were places where they themselves would like to eat, Nick and a family friend made a trip to the capital, offering bemused chefs samples of smoked venison on buttered brown bread, hastily prepared between visits in the back of the car. This perhaps unconventional marketing approach paid off, and today the meat is sold through various restaurants as well as the farm shop where new Layer Marney specialities are sausages and bacon.

The Charringtons point out that their products are highly complementary. Although the pork may be fatty, the venison is lean and whilst both Nick and Sheila firmly believe that 'you are what you eat', they would also hold that a little of what you fancy can do you no harm at all. Customers who appreciate being able to see – literally – where their meat has come from have proved the Charringtons right in their approach: the future at Layer Marney looks as if it will be just as interesting as the past.

Sheila recommends that the novice sausage-maker take the mixture to your local butcher who, by arrangement, can fill and knot the skins for you. She says it is very important to make friends with your butcher because butchers do not make sausages every day; a small independent butcher will probably make them once a week, and you will have to ask him nicely if he will case your mixture when he has done his own.

For those who case their own sausage, Sheila also recommends the use of natural sausage skins and, most importantly, fresh herbs for the mixture. Both the following recipes will make about 5.5 kg (11 lb) sausages – *see* page 9 for a general note on sausage quantities. The sausages can be frozen.

Venison and Herb Chipolatas

5 kg (10 lb) minced venison
720 g (1½ lb) dried breadcrumbs or rusk
3 teaspoons salt
3 teaspoons black pepper
90 g (3 oz) tarragon, finely chopped
600 ml (1 pint) water

Pork Sausages with Herbs

Less rusk, or filler, is required for this recipe since pork is not as strong a meat as venison. Sheila recommends that free-range or organic pork should be used if at all possible since she believes the flavour is more noticeably different with pork than any other meat. It is not necessary to buy an expensive cut of meat from your butcher – shoulder or flank would be fine.

5 kg (10 lb) minced pork
480 g (1 lb) dried breadcrumbs or rusk
3 teaspoons salt
3 teaspoons pepper
30 g (1 oz) parsley, finely chopped
45 g (1½ oz) chives, finely chopped
400 mls (⅔ pint) water

The cooking instructions for both are as follows:

Mix the ingredients thoroughly, slowly adding water. Only add enough water to soak up the breadcrumbs/rusk and don't allow the mixture to become sloppy. Skin and knot and allow to hang for 12 hours.

General note about sausages
The reason the sausages need to hang is because you have to wet the mixture to get it into the skins. Hanging lets this moisture drain out; otherwise, the sausages would spit when cooking. If you take your mixture to your butcher to case, he may or may not hang them for you, depending on when you pick them up. If the butcher has hung them, you need not; they only need hanging once.

John and Christian Curtis

Bonchester Bridge, Roxburghshire

Gave up making cheese in September 1998 because of goat. persecution

The story of John and Christian Curtis and their Bonchester cheese is the classic tale of late-twentieth-century rural life. Easter Weens is a 40-acre farm on what had once been part of the family estate. Situated in the valley of the River Rule in the Scottish Borders, it is at once idyllic countryside and a classified 'de-populated area', John and Christian took on the challenge of trying to make a living from Easter Weens in 1978. Realising they had to capitalise on the exquisite setting, they built holiday chalets. This turned out to be a shrewder move than they knew since Saturday (change-over day) was the only day when they were really busy, leaving the other six free for experimentation.

They planted up ½ acre of Pick Your Own soft fruit and then discovered a demand from pickers for cream to go with them. Always ready to try something new, they bought two Jersey cows. But cream was found to be a seasonal market, butter unprofitable and yogurt restricted by the cost of refrigerated transport. It was only then that cheese presented itself as a product with a satisfactorily long shelf-life as well as something (unlike yogurt) for which customers are prepared to pay significantly more for a significantly superior product.

Bonchester, a Camembert-type cheese which does full justice to the rich Jersey milk, has now been joined by two other varieties, Belle d'Ecosse and Teviotdale, and John and Christian are heavily involved with the Specialist Cheesemakers' Association. 'At Easter Weens, we don't see other farmhouse cheesemakers as competition,' John explains simply. 'Without them, the specialist shops we supply wouldn't be able to offer the variety of products that makes them interesting and attractive to customers.'

In the fever of activity which is Easter Weens today, with its increased acreage, its expanded herd and its purpose-built dairy and cheese rooms, it's surprising that breakfast is a fixed point in the day. 'We may not have a cooked breakfast, but we always sit down properly,' says Christian firmly. 'We have muesli with fresh banana, apple or, in summer, the ultimate luxury – nectarines and figs from the greenhouse. On special occasions I roast green coffee beans in a really heavy, very old frying pan on the Aga, then grind them to make the most delicious coffee. The whole house fills with the smell and it reminds me of my childhood in Ethiopia where coffee was always freshly roasted.'

Cheese, of course, and Selkirk bannock were on the table when 'On Your Farm' visited. The ripe smell of Bonchester mingled with the yeasty, fruited bread – and that of freshly roasted coffee.

Selkirk Bannock
Makes one 9-in round bannock

Christian Curtis freely admits that her cooking owes a debt of gratitude to Theodora Fitzgibbon who has done so much to promote Scottish produce and traditional recipes. Christian's Selkirk Bannock is based on a recipe from Theodora Fitzgibbon's book, *A Taste of Scotland*. Although candied peel is an optional extra in a bannock, Christian omits it for the traditional taste.

120 g (4 oz) butter
120 g (4 oz) lard
300 ml (½ pint) milk, warmed but not hot
30 g (1 oz) fresh yeast
½ teaspoon granulated sugar
960 g (2 lb) plain flour
240 g (8 oz) caster sugar
480 g (1 lb) sultanas or seedless raisins
milk and sugar for glazing

Melt the butter and lard in a saucepan and add the previously warmed milk. Cream the yeast with the granulated sugar and add to the pan.

Sift the flour into a large bowl, make a well in the centre and pour on the liquid from the pan. With a wooden spoon, make a batter, drawing the flour in from round the sides. Cover with a cloth and leave in a warm place for about 1 hour, until the mixture has doubled in size.

Warm the caster sugar by spreading it on a baking sheet and placing in a warm oven. Knead the bannock, add the warmed sugar and the raisins, and knead again for about 5 minutes. Pat into a flattish round, cover with a cloth and leave it in a warm place for a further 45 minutes. Then bake in a pre-heated oven at 180°C/350°F/Gas Mark 4 for 1 hour.

Remove from the oven, glaze the top with about a tablespoon of milk and a teaspoon of sugar which you have warmed together, and return the bannock to the oven for a further 30 minutes, or until browned.

Test with a knife or skewer inserted into the middle: if the implement comes out clean, the bannock is cooked. The bottom will also sound hollow when tapped. This is delicious eaten either warm or cold, with butter.

Matt and Mary Dempsey

Griffenrath, Co. Kildare

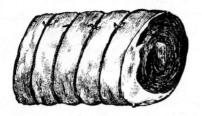

Mary and Matt Dempsey broke all the 'On Your Farm' rules: they called it 'brunch' but Mary's leek and potato soup followed by roast beef was, in truth, far less of a late breakfast than an early lunch, and one to which Oliver Walston did full justice.

Matt is the Editor of the *Irish Farmer's Journal* and though desk-bound for much of his time, he still takes enormous pleasure in his own arable farm and, in particular, his kitchen garden. It is a tradition in his family, adhered to by his mother and by Mary, that 'if you keep the family well fed, doctor's bills are minimal'. (Since the Dempseys have nine children, this is an important consideration.)

But as well as being a sensible financial stricture, this places the Dempseys firmly within a strong Irish tradition, not just of owner-occupiers but of a desire to be in touch with the land, even when the city lifestyle encroaches. Mary's father was a Dublin publican but, out the back, among the beer crates, he had rows and rows of neatly-hoed potatoes and onions, as well as the family cow and chickens. Does it really all hark back to a national sense of insecurity resulting from the great potato famine?

Theories abound: all Matt will say is that there is nothing like the taste of home-grown vegetables. The arrival of the first Cypriot new potatoes in the shops is, he says, cause for commiseration not celebration in his house. Mary bakes all her own bread, keeps chickens and grows soft fruits and slender pink stems of rhubarb for tarts, pies and fools all summer long. Come late August and September, the Dempseys are to be found raiding 'nature's larder' for windfall apples, blackberries and sloes. Jewel-coloured jellies and pale-crusted pies sustain them throughout the winter.

If Matt can ever be lured away on holiday from the twin demands of the farm and the *Journal*, he doesn't leave his *raison d'être* behind. His favourite holiday ever was the one which took in George Washington's old home on the banks of the Potomac river where he drooled over the immaculate vegetable garden containing all the old American Indian varieties. As Matt says categorically: 'There is nothing as mentally satisfying as a well-maintained vegetable garden. It is the heart of the home.'

Mary's Leek and Potato Soup
Serves 6

60 g (2 oz) butter
3–4 leeks, washed and sliced
6 medium (old) potatoes, peeled and cut into dice

    900 ml (1½ pints) home-made chicken stock
    salt and pepper
    150 ml (¼ pint) milk, to taste

Melt the butter in a large heavy saucepan. When it foams, add the leeks and potatoes and turn in the butter until well coated. Sprinkle with salt and pepper. Cover the pan to keep in the steam and sweat until the vegetables are soft but not coloured. Add the chicken stock and gently boil until the vegetables are just cooked. Liquidise. Taste and adjust seasoning accordingly. Add milk to taste and serve with home-made bread and Irish butter.

Roast Beef à La Griffenrath

Go to your local butcher and order the first rib of the forequarter of prime heifer beef, the one next to the sirloin. Ask for it to be boned and rolled – it should be about 2.5 kg–3 kg (5–6 lb) in weight.

Rub in olive oil and then cook in the hot oven of the Aga, or roast at 200°C/400°F/Gas Mark 6 for the first half hour. Then remove it to the bottom (baking) oven of the Aga or reduce the heat of a conventional oven to 180°C/350°F/Gas Mark 4 for the remaining time.

The recommended overall cooking times are 15 minutes to the .5 kg (1 lb), plus 15 minutes over, for rare meat; in the same way, 20 minutes for medium meat, and 25 minutes for well-done meat.

Serve with creamed horseradish, mustard and gravy.

John and Nichola Fletcher

Auchtermuchty, Fife

If you've never tasted venison before and are nervous about how to cook it, maybe the first piece you buy should be from Fletchers of Auchtermuchty. John and Nichola's after-sales service is such that they've even had people telephoning for advice when the meat is in the oven: with one of them talking the nervous chef through it's hard to see how even the most inept cook could fail.

Deer and venison are John and Nichola's life and work – and if that sounds in any way narrow, they also had a pretty full pre-deer existence as vet and jeweller-designer/silversmith respectively. Since 1973, however, their creativity has been concentrated on the farmed red deer which graze the hills of the Reediehill Deer Farm and in marketing the venison they produce: Nichola's stated ambition is to make it available to every discerning eater in Britain.

Wild venison can be of variable quality: the meat is essentially a by-product of a sporting industry and wild deer can be very thin or old animals – a selective cull. The Fletchers' farm imitates the idea of a medieval deer park. The animals are reared simply and healthily and are dispatched humanely at close quarters in prime condition. The carcases are hung for 2–3 weeks (the equivalent of hanging beef for 8–10 weeks). The meat, already lean, therefore acquires a superb, mature flavour and texture. Some of the meat is also made into sausages, venison burgers and haggis: Nichola has channelled her artistic leanings into devising venison recipes and writing and illustrating cookery books.

There is no doubt that John and Nichola could earn more if they were prepared to adulterate their products. Instead, everything they make is the sort of food that they would want to – and do – eat themselves. The most important ingredient, Nichola feels, is integrity. 'Otherwise we wouldn't feel right selling them.'

Venison and Tomato Breakfast Sausage
Makes 10–16 sausages

480 g (1 lb) venison mince
90 g (3 oz) minced pork belly
   or 4 tablespoons vegetable oil
60 g (2 oz) medium oatmeal
1 small tin chopped tomatoes
   or 240 g (½ lb) cherry tomatoes
salt, pepper, nutmeg, ginger, oregano

This is a loose adaptation of one of John and Nichola's sausage recipes which you can make without a sausage filler and casings. They are best made the night before so that they hold together. Nichola recommends cherry tomatoes for flavour. If these are not available, tinned work better than any other fresh tomato.

Mix together the venison, pork belly (or oil), oatmeal, and enough chopped tomatoes to bind the mixture softly, bearing in mind it will stiffen slightly overnight. Mix together a teaspoon of salt, 12 turns of a black pepper grinder, a pinch each of nutmeg and ginger, and a large pinch of oregano. Then scatter this over the mixture and thoroughly amalgamate.

Divide the mixture into 16 (or 10 if you like plumper sausages) and roll into sausages. Leave overnight to firm, or freeze for later use. You may bake them or fry them, but if frying, dust them with flour first.

Rowan Jelly
Makes about 20 × 250 g (½ pt) jars

3 kg (7 lb) (a carrier-bagful) Rowan sprigs – berries, stalk and all about 3 kg (7 lbs) granulated sugar
½ bottle pectin (optional)

When picking the rowan sprigs, respect the tree by making sure you don't damage the bud which is next year's growth. Remove only the leaves from the clusters of rowan berries. Put all the rest, stalks and all, into a big pan and cover with water until the berries start to float. Bring to the boil and simmer for at least an hour, then use a potato masher to turn the berries into a thick pulp. Strain through a jelly bag. (The pulp left over, Nichola suggests, makes an excellent mulch for raspberry canes and the birds love the seeds.)

Measure out the juice into the cleaned jelly pan, and for every 600 ml (1 pint) of juice, add 480 g (1 lb) sugar. Dissolve, then boil rapidly until set (anything from 10–40 minutes). If desperate, or if you want a firmer jelly, add ½ bottle of pectin before pouring into the jars.

John Fletcher's Bitter Marmalade

This is John's father's recipe and he makes it for old time's sake and because he can't find any as good in the shops. John will only use Seville oranges, the fruit of the wild orange tree, available in January. (Even Shakespeare knew they were bitter and punned with them – 'as Seville as an orange'.)

John and Nichola admit that, on first reading, their recipe may not sound much different from the standard marmalade recipe, but say that, every time they make it, they marvel at the result. They think it must be a happy combination of the proportions and the method – perhaps the secret is leaving the peel and water overnight to draw out extra flavours. They describe the result as a 'uniquely tangy, bittersweet marmalade, never insipid and very more-ish'.

To fill about 15 × 450g (1lb) jars
   3 kg (7 lb) Seville oranges
   2.75 litres (5 pints) water
   3 kg (7 lb) granulated sugar

The oranges are easy to peel. Chop the peel; I use a food processor as it is very quick and I am more concerned about the flavour than the symmetry. Use your fingers to locate and remove the numerous pips in the flesh – tedious. Tie the pips up in a bit of muslin and suspend them in the (now chopped) flesh overnight. Meanwhile, put the chopped peel and water in a covered pan in a warm place overnight to infuse. (If you have an Aga/Rayburn or similar, the cool oven is perfect. If you do not, the best place is near a warm radiator or in the airing cupboard.)

Next day, amalgamate the peel and water with the flesh in a preserving pan. Suspend the bag of pips in the marmalade from a string tied to the handle. Bring to the boil, and boil rapidly until setting point is reached. Squeeze the bag of pips to extract all the pectin. Allow to cool slightly before putting into warmed jars.

Bottle enough for eleven months so you will run out and be keen enough to make some more the following January.

Alan and Jackie Gear

Ryton Organic Gardens, Coventry

Sewage sludge doesn't sound the most promising beginning for what turned out to be a fruitful partnership, but it was the subject of a long correspondence between Jackie Gear and the environmentalist and scientist Lawrence Hills, founder of the Henry Doubleday Research Association. When Lawrence later advertised for two young scientists to help him on the HDRA's organic research station, Jackie and Alan's applications were in more quickly than you can say 'salary negotiable' – which it wasn't, because there was no remuneration at all. They thankfully gave up their jobs, however (Jackie specialised in water pollution control and Alan was a civil engineer), and willingly traded in their Betjemanesque semi-detached, clean cuffs and notional Cortina for life in a caravan because, as Jackie says, 'We wanted to change our whole lifestyle to reflect our environmental beliefs.'

That was in 1973. Nearly twenty-five years later, the Gears are joint directors of the HDRA whose activities and membership have grown enormously. It is still their fundamental belief that a sustainable future depends on mankind's return to a more natural way of life, in which the soil, as the fount of fertility, is treated with respect. More and more people, says Jackie, want agricultural and horticultural systems to be managed in an environmentally friendly way, leading to pure, wholesome food: scare stories about levels of pesticide residues in vegetables show that the debate and the concerns over intensive agriculture have moved beyond the animal welfare arena.

Jackie and Alan are lucky: Ryton Gardens runs an organic restaurant and shop so organic food is easy to come by. Though weekdays are frantically busy, Jackie and Alan do slow down on Sundays when they can indulge in a proper breakfast. 'As a Welsh girl,' says Jackie, 'my absolute favourite is laverbread and organic bacon. I was spoilt in my younger days by having access to Swansea market which is full of local produce from the Gower peninsular – butter, wholewheat breads, superb vegetables, home-cured ham and last, but not least, cockles and laverbread.

'Words cannot describe how wonderful laverbread is, rolled in oatmeal and fried in bacon fat – a true gastronomic experience, especially when it's accompanied by my home-made organic bread which I make with freshly-ground flour.'

Alan and Jackie's Organic Breakfast
For 2 people

6 rashers best back bacon
240 g (½ lb) fresh laverbread (tinned is second best)
2 free range eggs
virgin olive oil for frying
several slices wholewheat bread
best Welsh butter

Fry the bacon until crisp and keep warm. Toss the laverbread in oatmeal so it makes a big patty. Fry this in the bacon fat until it is heated through. In a separate pan, fry the eggs – a soft yolk is best. Serve everything on warmed plates, with home-made bread and butter to mop up the juices.

Note Anne Petch gives instructions on how to clean fresh laver on page 85. The recipe Jackie uses for her home-made bread is similar to that given by Patrick Holden on page 53.

Welsh Cakes

To round off this scrumptious meal, and in keeping with Jackie's background, what better than a couple of Welsh cakes. Jackie says that the smell of these, hot, takes her right back to her grandmother's kitchen, but she adds that she departs from tradition to make a wholemeal version, the traditional ingredients being, as she puts it, 'white and deadly'.

Ideally you need a bakestone or griddle but a heavy pan or skillet will do. Use organic ingredients whenever possible.

To make 20 Welsh cakes

    300 g (10 oz) best Welsh butter
    480 g (1 lb) self-raising flour (half white, half
      wholemeal)
    180 g (6 oz) light muscovado sugar
    180 g (6 oz) sultanas and currants, mixed
    1 egg (size 3/4)
    milk to bind
    salt

Rub the butter into the flour in a large bowl and add the sugar and dried fruit, then mix in the beaten egg, and a little salt. Add enough milk to make a dough-like shortcrust pastry. Don't handle this more than necessary. Turn out onto a well-floured surface, roll out and cut into 3-inch rounds that are ½ inch thick.

Place the rounds on a hot, lightly greased bakestone, or in a greased heavy frying pan or skillet, and cook for 3–4 minutes on each side. Do not overcook them on too hot a bakestone, or they will be burnt on the outside and not cooked inside. It's easy to get the hang of it with just a little practice and well worth the effort.

Eat them warm, just as they are – avoiding, if possible, the temptation to eat too many.

Sue and Michael Gibson

Forres, Inverness-shire

When Sue and Michael Gibson took over a butcher's shop in their local town to process and sell meat from their own Highland cattle and other breeds of prime Scots beef, as well as venison, pork and lamb, they had no idea, they now admit, what they were taking on.

They had always killed their own animals from the farm, and an increasing number of people were approaching them, asking for half a lamb or a side of beef. A shop seemed a natural diversification, both a way of maximising profit and a way of putting their potential customers directly in touch with the source of what they would be eating. They had, Michael remembers ruefully, a 'ten-day honeymoon' before they realised what they had done: it took considerably longer to get the right staff in the shop, turn the sales graph around, and build up a business encompassing mail order, the wholesale trade and the hotel and restaurant business as well as the all-important shop.

For their meat, the Gibsons are anxious to use only

native Scottish breeds: grass-fed cattle which have matured naturally. (The Gibsons' own cattle are never killed before they reach two years of age, by which time natural marbling of the flesh has occurred which so improves the flavour. In post-BSE Britain, however, this leaves them a very small window in which to operate.) Barley and grain, in Michael's opinion, are not the ideal food for cattle, leading to a paler colour and a more wobbly, jelly-like texture to the flesh than that found in grass-fed beef. He predicts that people who have not eliminated beef from their diet will increasingly want to know exactly where it has come from and the method of rearing: he was greatly encouraged during the BSE scare to find that sales (of prime cuts, at least) actually increased.

This could well be because the Gibsons have fostered an atmosphere of trust between themselves and their customers. The company philosophy is not just that the customer is always right but that no two customers are the same. Instead of being hung with butchered cuts, the shop is spartan: most of the meat is kept in the fridge and is cut to order. As a result, says Michael, they have the puniest window display in town – but the tastiest meat.

Potted Hough

Sue Gibson says she thought long and hard about providing a traditional breakfast recipe for black pudding but decided that the instruction to acquire a couple of pints of blood might put people off. Similarly the 'first take a sheep's stomach' aspect of haggis was a probable turn-off. She chose, therefore, this recipe for potted hough, equally traditional Scottish fare. Hough (pronounced 'hoch') is basically shin of beef, one of the poorer cuts, though it can be delicious when cooked slowly in stew. This recipe results in a jellied dish which extracts all the goodness from the meat.

1 kg (2 lb) hough
1 knap bone (ask your butcher!)
4 whole cloves
salt and pepper

Place the hough, bone and cloves in a large saucepan. Cover with cold water and bring to the boil. Skim, then simmer gently for 6 hours. Strain the stock, leave until cold and remove the fat. Mince the meat and add it to the stock. Bring it to the boil again, season with salt and freshly-ground black pepper and let it stand for ½ hour. Stir, then pour into wetted ring moulds. Turn out as required, and surround with salad leaves.

Malcolm and Rowena Harrison

Hoskins, West New Britain

It's a long way from being a School Meals supervisor in Harrogate to teaching basic nutrition to South Sea islanders but it's the journey which Rowena Harrison made when her husband Malcolm accepted a post with VSO on the island of West New Britain, in Papua New Guinea. A crash course in pidgin was also a crash course in the local cuisine: despite the availability of fresh produce, Rowena was horrified to find that the basic diet of the islanders was tinned fish, rice and *kumu* (greens), supplemented with flour balls (flour, water, sugar and salt mixed to a paste and deep-fried) and the equally un-nutritious grated *cassava* (from which tapioca is made) cooked in coconut milk: when transported in banana leaves, this is the local equivalent of fast food.

Further researches revealed that the islanders, lacking electricity, had evolved sustainable ways of cooking, principally by heating stones in a fire, dropping them in a hole in the ground and using the ensuing oven to bake meat, fish or, more usually, vegetables – chiefly the *kaukau* or sweet potato – basted with coconut milk and wrapped in banana leaves. The result, though slightly more interesting than flour balls, was still primarily a starchy, high-carbohydrate 'filler'. The distended bellies of the children and the malnutrition amongst the women (lowest in the pecking order when it comes to food) were the two most acute problems which Rowena had to tackle.

Among her suggestions were adding a meat or fish filling to the flour balls, and coming up with alternative 'packed lunches' for schoolchildren. However, the *kaukau* cakes which were served to presenter Quentin Seddon when he breakfasted with the Harrisons when they were on leave in England were a true taste of the Pacific. Luckily, the Harrisons had not contrived to bring home any of Papua New Guinea's chief delicacy: the slugs which grow on the sago tree.

Kaukau Cake
To make 10 cakes

> 120 g (4 oz) plain flour
> 1 teaspoon of baking powder
> 2 level tablespoons of sugar
> 90 g (3 oz) cooked kaukau (sweet potato)
> 2 level tablespoons of margarine
> 1 level tablespoon of milk
> pinch of salt

To cook kaukau, slice the peeled vegetable and cook as normal for about 20 minutes until it is soft and mushy; drain. Sift the flour and baking powder into a bowl and add sugar. Mash the cooked kaukau with margarine, milk and salt. Add the kaukau to the flour mixture and mix well with a wooden spoon to a soft dough. Take small spoonfuls of dough, roll them into balls and place on a greased oven tray. Flatten them lightly with a fork and bake in a moderate oven (180°C/350°F/ Gas Mark 4) for 15 minutes or until golden brown. They are best served warm and no accompaniment is needed.

Henry Head

Heacham, Norfolk

Lavender is the herb of cleanliness and calm. When you think that some animal keepers have reputedly found that it will work on lions and tigers, making them quite docile, it's surprising that it is not more widely used in human society – just think of the beneficial effects in the average office, not to mention the family home...

If they think of using lavender at all, most people would turn to the essential oil, widely used in aromatherapy. But just because it is known primarily for its scent, don't think it cannot also enhance the taste of food. After all, as Henry Head, whose family has been growing lavender for over forty years, points out, we use other scented plants in food. Thyme, rosemary and sage are some of the most popular and fragrant flavourings we know; candied violets and angelica are not uncommon and edible flowers like the nasturtium occasionally turn up in the salad bowl. So why are we so nervous of lavender in the kitchen?

Years ago (and the history of lavender in this country may even pre-date the Romans), cooks had to use whatever was available to flavour food which, at best, was bland; at worst, actually 'off'. In Provence, lavender turns up regularly in roasts, casseroles and vinegars. To Henry Head, its culinary applications are obvious – but, he concedes, if you are wary of using the stronger-scented flowers, try the leaves which add a pleasant, if puzzling, aroma to fish, duck, chicken, lamb or pork.

Despite his paeons of praise for lavender in cooking, when the Heads served sizzling Yarmouth bloaters for breakfast, there wasn't a sprig of lavender in sight – just the robust taste of the sea!

Yarmouth Bloaters
One bloater per person

Cut off heads, tails and fins and remove the backbones. With a sharp knife make three slashes along one side of each fish. Brush with a little melted butter or oil. Very lightly grill the bloaters on both sides then fill the slashes with a little French mustard. Add extra melted butter and flash back under the hot grill to brown.

Several lavender items are served in the Norfolk Lavender Tearoom. They range from lavender maids of honour to lavender chutney – but not all would be suitable for breakfast! The following are three recommendations from the Tearoom:

47

Lavender Tea

Add 2 or 3 flower heads of dried lavender to your favourite tea in your tea caddy. This will impart a delicious 'extra' to your brew.

Lavender Jelly

- 3 kg (6 lb) cooking apples
- 3 litres (5 pints) water
- 2.25 kg (5 lbs) sugar
- 3 handfuls (approx) lavender flowers (¾ of a large teacup)
- 5 tablespoons lemon juice

Wash the apples and chop them, including the peel and core. Put the fruit into a preserving pan with the water and bring to the boil. Simmer until pulpy – about 30 minutes. Pour into a jelly bag and leave overnight to drip without disturbance.

The next day, measure the drained juice and add 500 g (1 lb) sugar to every 600 ml (1 pint) of juice. Place in a pan and bring to the boil with the lavender. Boil steadily for about 20 minutes until the setting point is reached. Skim off the surface scum and then stir in the lemon juice. Pour into warmed sterilised jars and cover. Delicious on bread and butter, or scones.

Lavender Marmalade

 1 kg (2¼ lb) Seville oranges
 1 lemon
 2.3 litres (3¾ pints) water
 2 kg (4½ lb) preserving sugar
 30 g (1 oz) lavender flowers (dried and tied in a
    muslin bag)

Being so light, lavender is hard to weigh accurately. A volume measure is a good alternative. If you tip the flowers into a measuring jug to the 200 ml line, you will have about 30 g = 1 oz.

Cut the fruit in half, extract the juice and pips, shred the peel as you like it. If the pith is thick, remove some. Put the peel, juice and water into a pan, add pips in a muslin bag and bring to the boil. Simmer gently for approximately 1½ hours or until the peel is tender. Squeeze the bag of pips to release any liquid and remove. Stir in the sugar (previously warmed on a baking tray in a low oven for a few minutes) over a gentle heat until dissolved. Add the lavender in a muslin bag and bring the mixture to a fast boil for 10 minutes. Press the juice from the lavender bag and remove. Continue a fast boil until setting point is reached. Leave to stand for ½ hour, stir, turn into warm, dry, sterilised jars and cover to make airtight.

Natalie Hodgson

Bridgnorth, Shropshire

All bees ask for in order to make honey is pollen and sun – such easy creatures to please, says Natalie Hodgson, and such a delicious by-product. The honey produced by the bees in her twenty hives is not, however, her main crop: Natalie owns the only Pick Your Own lavender farm in the country. In today's sophisticated market, however, some entertainment for the visitors is deemed necessary. Scorning bouncy castles and barbecue areas, Natalie has instead grouped her bee hives into a village, representing a row of shops, the church, the pub and the cottages at Numbers 1, 2 and 3 Pollen Row.

Natalie admits that the taste of lavender in the resultant honey is somewhat elusive: it is not as strong a presence as, say, the orange blossom or cotton flowers found in Israeli honey or, indeed, that produced from oilseed rape. As a cooking ingredient, honey is the basis of many sweet and savoury recipes, as well as the foundation for so-called 'weak beer' and mead. It is a genuine whole food and, some say, being a monosaccharide, is easier to digest than sugar, hence its reputation for healthiness. As for claims that it prolongs life, Natalie demurs. But after hearing of her life experiences, which have encompassed broadcasting wartime propaganda, a career in the Foreign Office, having three children and serving as a County Councillor, one begins to wonder. Oh, and she's recently taken up waterskiing. Natalie is eighty-six years old . . .

Gammon with Honey and Mustard Sauce
Per serving

  1 240 g (8 oz) gammon steak weighing 180 g–240 g
  (6–8 oz)
  30 g (1 oz) butter
  2 tablespoons olive or vegetable oil
  2 tablespoons honey, warmed
  1 tablespoon wholegrain mustard
  2 teaspoons white wine vinegar
  salt and pepper to taste

Heat butter and oil until foaming and add the gammon steak. Sear quickly on both sides then reduce the heat. Add all the other ingredients and mix to make a smooth sauce. Season to taste but remember the gammon is itself salty. Allow to simmer for 10–15 minutes. Remove the gammon to a warm serving plate. Reduce the sauce by boiling rapidly, then pour over the gammon and serve.

Patrick Holden

City of Bristol

Patrick Holden claims that he has always been a fairly unfussy eater but, as an inevitable by-product of his work as Director of the Soil Association, he has read and digested more about food, farming and production methods than can possibly be good for him. As chief spokesman for the organic movement for many years, he has often been asked to comment on the latest findings of official committees, scientific bodies and pressure groups as well as anecdotal evidence from consumers. It has led him to an unshakeable belief that the nutritional quality of food – meat and vegetables, in particular – has a fundamental effect on human health. He does not eat any meat which has not been organically produced and is thus hormone- and chemical-free, and looks for vegetables which have been organically grown, locally produced and are therefore in season.

But in case that makes him sound terribly earnest, Patrick believes that the most important reason to eat organically is because it makes you feel good. 'There is nothing I know quite so satisfying as to eat a meal which has been well prepared with organic ingredients grown in the garden or on the farm where you live. After eating such a meal, one understands profoundly the meaning of the relationship between food quality and human health.'

Organic Wholewheat Bread

The kneading of bread is not essential and the 'wet' method, where rather more water than usual is used and the dough is simply mixed in the bowl before being placed in the tins, can produce an equally acceptable (and possibly more nutritious) loaf in less time.

This is a variation of the recipe for no-knead bread promoted by Doris Grant and included in her book *Your Daily Bread*, which was published in 1944, two years before the Soil Association was founded.

- 1.75 kg (3½ lb) English stone-ground wholewheat flour
- 30 g (1 oz) sea salt, Maldon salt or ordinary salt
- 30 g (1 oz) yeast (or up to 120 g/4 oz for extra food value)
- 30 g (1 oz) sugar, preferably Barbados muscovado cane sugar
- 1.3 litres (2¼ pints) water at blood heat

Mix the flour with the salt in a large basin and warm it in a low oven or over a low gas flame so that the yeast will work more quickly.

Crumble the yeast into a pudding basin, add the sugar and 150 ml (¼ pint) of the lukewarm water. Leave for 10 minutes to froth up; then stir to dissolve the sugar. Pour this yeasty liquid into the basin of warm flour, add the rest of the warm water, then stir the whole with a wooden spoon until the flour is evenly wetted. The resulting dough should be wet enough to be slippery; most bread is too dry.

Grease the insides of three 1 kg (2 lb) tins and warm them well. Spoon the dough into the warmed tins, put them in a warm place (or in a very low oven), cover with a cloth and leave for about 20 minutes to rise by about one-third. Then bake them in an oven, pre-heated to 200°C/400°F/Gas Mark 6 for 45 minutes to 1 hour.

Bread making is trial and error and only experience will teach you how long to allow the loaves to rise before baking. If left too long, the loaf will be spongy, too short a time and the loaf will be too denselytextured.

When baked, tap the top crust with your knuckles. It should sound hollow. Turn the loaves out to cool, upside down on a wire tray. If you can't get the loaves out of the tins, leave them for another 10 minutes or so. Like all bread, these loaves are best kept for 24 hours before eating.

Carmel Kehoe

Ennis, Co. Clare

Although Sister Carmel belongs to the religious community called the Sisters of Saint John of God, she has chosen to live on her own. 'I find it easier to negotiate life that way,' she says simply. But other people are, and always have been, a large part of her life. For years she was involved in rural resettlement: people she met then have become and remained friends.

Visitors to her home have to find their way through the colourful clutter which abounds: pieces of drift wood, bog deal and bog oak, lumps of granite and multi-coloured slate and marble. Paintings, pottery, collage, sketches and photographs cover the walls. From the ceilings hang mobiles of birds and clowns: teddy bears of varying colour, shapes and sizes lurk behind cushions and curtains. 'All in all,' she admits cheerily, 'this is a place of chaos – but many people are happy to come here to talk, to cry, to laugh, to pray or just to say hello.'

Sister Carmel doesn't confine the blessing of the Eucharist to merely receiving communion at Mass. 'Sitting together with people and just chatting or listening or having a meal can be a real time of communion,' she says. 'People would never leave here without at least the offer of a cup of tea. Hospitality is very much part of my nature, of my culture. It is also one of the charismas of the Sisters of Saint John of God. I know how badly I need nourishment for both the body and soul – I think of the Eucharist as food for the journey.'

Sister Carmel's Porridge

Sister Carmel comments that, in years gone by, prisoners were given large amounts of porridge to eat. Since this was often their only means of sustenance, likes or dislikes rarely featured and prisoners ate in abundance. Consequently, they left prison looking well nourished. Sister Carmel thought that 'On Your Farm' presenter Oliver Walston looked too well-cared for to need building up, but she served him porridge anyway which he ate, she adds, 'with apparent relish'. No book of breakfast recipes would be complete without one for porridge.

    1 cupful of oatlets/medium oatmeal
    3 cupfuls of cold water or milk
    salt
    sugar

Steep oatmeal in water or milk overnight. Bring to the boil, stirring all the time. Add a pinch of salt and a teaspoon of sugar. Allow to simmer for 20 minutes. Serve piping hot.

As a change, omit the sugar and use good country honey as a sweetener instead; maybe a flower honey. It should be stirred in at the end.

Andrew Lane and John Noble

Cairndow, Argyllshire

Samuel Johnson used to feed them to his cat: there was nothing cheaper. In Victorian times, they were two a penny – literally. So why, now, do oysters have the image of being a luxury indulged in by the very rich?

Andrew Lane and John Noble not only have the answers – pollution and over-fishing – but the determination to reverse the trend. At the seafood restaurant attached to their fish smokery and shop at the head of Loch Fyne, the prices are reasonable and the clientèle as likely to be a family in climbing boots as a party in business suits. There is no hushed, reverential atmosphere, either: John wants his customers to partake of their food with lip-smacking relish: 'To enjoy seafood you have to get stuck in, using your hands to pull the crabs apart. You can't be prim and proper when you're whacking into a plate of langoustines with garlic butter.'

John and Andrew see it as their vocation to restore the oyster to its rightful place in Britain's gastronomic heritage: as the original fast food. When the Oyster Bar was opened at Grand Central Station in New York at the turn of the century, it was to provide commuters with a quick snack. The tempting option of half a dozen oysters or a slice of smoked salmon and a glass of chilled white wine could, perhaps, remove the infamous British Rail sandwich from the memory once and for all.

Grilled Kippers

John favours grilling rather than poaching kippers because of the crispy texture that results. He has no magic remedy for ridding the house of the ensuing smell: in fact, he likes it.

Grill your kippers with the skin side uppermost until the skin creases and the kipper begins to bend towards the heat. Serve with a knob of butter.

Angels on Horseback

Remove fresh oysters from their shell. Wrap them in thinly-cut smoked bacon and grill until the bacon begins to crisp. Serve on or with buttered toast. For breakfast, serve 6–8 per person, depending on what else is served; 8 per person as a savoury.

Joy Larkcom and Don Pollard

Diss, Norfolk

One of Joy Larkcom's earliest memories is of helping her father, newly returned from the war, in the garden: her task was to pick out the wireworms and take them to the hens. As Quentin Seddon pointed out at breakfast, this could have put her off gardening for life, but happily it didn't and Joy went on to train in horticulture. Various careers got in the way (including writing on careers for the *Observer*) but by the time she had met Don and started a family, the call of the soil from the Fens was seeping into her London life. They moved out to Ely and got an allotment.

Time spent with runner beans and purple sprouting was limited, however. Joy was busy establishing herself as a journalist on *Garden News*, for which she wrote a column on unusual vegetables – 'queer gear' or 'exotics' as they are known in the trade. Joy is quick to point out that what was unusual then is quite commonplace now but her interest was aroused. Her desk groaned with seed company catalogues as she researched the availability of lost or forgotten varieties.

Finally, in 1976, packing the uncomplaining Don and their two children, then aged five and seven, into a caravan, the whole family set off to travel for a year around Europe, determined to root out – literally, if necessary – vegetables which had fallen from grace, and certainly from British tables.

What they found, as well as antique varieties, were indigenous specialities never before seen in Britain. In fact, Joy is probably single-handedly responsible for the upsurge of interest in this country in *lollo rosso* lettuce (the blowsy variety the Italians named after the amply-endowed Gina Lollobrigida), not to mention *radicchio* (red chicory) and, following a latertrip which took her to Japan and China on a seed-collection mission, Oriental vegetables.

Joy's 'breakfast' table was as much a feast for the eyes as for the tastebuds: she described it as 'breakfast from the borders'. Ornamental cabbage, several different types of lettuce and tomato (such as the yellow tomato and the heirloom 'oxheart' variety), glossy aubergine and three types of pepper, along with edible flowers, made the salad bowl more like a flower arrangement. Joy recommends adding the edible flowers – she uses borage, pot marigold and nasturtium – *after* the dressing to stop them becoming soggy. There were also melons, beetroot, sprouting seeds and, to top it all, a Chinese loofah plant – perfectly edible (and delicious) when young.

Don's Soda Bread

300 g (10 oz) white flour
330 g (11 oz) wholemeal flour
1 teaspoon salt
1 tablespoon bicarbonate of soda
1 tablespoon granulated sugar
600 ml (1 pint) milk
3 tablespoons natural live yogurt

Mix the white and wholemeal flour together in a bowl. Stir in the salt, bicarbonate of soda and sugar. Mix together milk and yogurt to 'sour' the milk. Add the 'soured' milk to the dry ingredients until quite a moist dough is made. Knead into a ball on a floured board. Cut a cross on top of the ball with a floured knife. Put in a deep, greased, round baking tin and sprinkle a little flour in the cross indentations. Bake in a hot oven (220°C/425°F/Gas Mark 7) for about 30–45 minutes.

Check to see if it is thoroughly baked by inserting a knife into the bread. If the knife is clean when withdrawn, then the bread is ready.

Salad Dressings with an Oriental Flavour

These dressings were developed for salads of Chinese vegetables such as pak choi, Chinese cabbage and mustard greens. They are also good with bean sprouts, Oriental radish and stem lettuce, with strongly flavoured greens like western cabbage and kales, and with cooked and cold vegetables such as potatoes and beetroot.

Sweet and sour dressing
Make a syrup by warming a tablespoon of sugar in a little warm water. Add lemon juice and salt until the required sweet/sour balance is achieved; you may need to add more sugar/lemon juice to achieve this balance. Mix with a tablespoon each of sesame oil (or tahini) and rice wine vinegar, a little light soy sauce, grated or finely-sliced fresh ginger and, finally, a pinch of sugar just before serving.

Chinese dressing
Blend together 2½ tablespoons of groundnut oil and 1 tablespoon of rice vinegar. Gradually stir in the following: 2 tablespoons finely-chopped shallots or green onions, 2 tablespoons thinly-sliced sweet peppers, 1 tablespoon ground sesame seeds, 1 tablespoon of mixed light soy sauce, sea salt and ground black pepper, and 1 chopped garlic glove.

Sesame seed dressing
Crush 2 tablespoons of sesame seeds. Add to them 1 tablespoon sugar, 1 tablespoon light soy sauce, 2 tablespoons rice vinegar and ½ teaspoon salt.

Hugh Lillingstone

Tamworth, Staffordshire

Hugh Lillingstone and Oliver Walston must have made a striking couple when they breakfasted together for 'On Your Farm'. What Oliver wore is, sadly, lost in the mists of time, but Hugh was sporting a cream linen suit with a rose in his buttonhole; the table was elegantly laid, and included strawberries and raspberries from the garden, as well as Hugh's own goats' and cows' curd cheese and his famous sour-dough bread.

Sour-dough is an alien concept to most people, but it could have no more articulate nor fervent champion than Hugh. The subject of bread, in fact, in any shape or form, is enough to provoke a passionate condemnation of most mass-processed pap – ('Don't talk to me about supermarkets! They make a dough that holds for six days at room temperature in Milton Keynes or somewhere and call it bread ...') – ora fascinating account of the beginnings of wheat cultivation and fermentation, which are shrouded in mystery – although we do know that all bread was sour-dough bread until the late eighteenth century.

For Hugh, bread is, quite simply, the staff of life and since, as far as he's concerned, there's a clear and demonstrable relationship between the quality of food and physical and mental health, he puts forward a compelling economic argument for improving our diet. 'The cheapest way to maintain human health is to provide quality food and this should be our highest priority. Unfortunately, money has become an end in itself and our food chain has become compromised.' But all is not lost, Hugh asserts, because with a little time, trouble and modest expense it is possible to buy or, even better, make at home, the staple food of many nations – bread.

Not everyone would wish to go to the lengths Hugh went to when setting up his bakery business. Discovering a disused igloo-shaped bread oven in the South of France, he had the numbered stones shipped back to England, brought a French baker over to teach the craft and *still* had to spend nine months cultivating a 'mother' which would give consistent results. Having got this far, a sharp frost caused him to lose the entire first batch of dough with which he had been satisfied, but Hugh was undeterred.

His chewy-textured and thick-crusted sour-dough bread is now sold plain or with added nuts, olives, or sun-dried tomatoes and mustard seed – and Hugh is still as excited by every batch as he was by the first.

Hugh Lillingstone's Sour-Dough Bread

Just as home-made yogurt needs a starter culture, so does sour-dough bread. There are many ways of making a starter including honey, grapes, or potato peelings, but the simplest is given below. The point about sour-dough, however, is that it is not an exact science. The process requires – and will repay – love and attention from the baker. First make the starter culture – known as 'mother', 'sponge' or 'sour'.

500 g (1 lb 2 oz) organic wholemeal flour
2 kg (4½ lb) organic white flour
1.7 litres (3 pints) water
25 g (¾ oz) salt

Mix and knead for 10 minutes until the dough is supple and elastic. Leave overnight, covered at room temperature. Then feed every day for five days with:

100 g (3½ oz) wholemeal flour
200 g (7 oz) white flour
200 ml (7 fl oz) water
pinch of salt

At the end of five days (after which time you will have *fifteen* times the amount you began with on day one, since the mixture will double in size every day), the culture is ready to use. One-third volume by weight of sour-dough replaces yeast in whatever recipe you choose – i.e. for 450 g/1 lb flour and 300 ml/½ pt milk and water, use 225 g/½ lb sour-dough.

Angus Maxwell Macdonald

Tayinloan, Argyllshire

Snails for breakfast? Not the usual fare, even for an 'On Your Farm' presenter, but when they are served up on the Kintyre peninsula on a crisp winter's day, with the Sound of Gigha glinting in the distance, and swilled down with a mug of tea rather than a glass of Chardonnay, who could refuse?

Angus Maxwell Macdonald was brought up on Kintyre but his horizons, both geographical and gastronomic, have never been limited. He comes from a family of adventurous eaters, and at an age when most children are demanding HulaHoop sandwiches, was tucking into frogs' legs and snails on family holidays in France. He marvels that there are still those uninitiated in the snail experience who would dismiss the idea of eating them as both 'creepy' and 'expensive'.

The *raison d'être* behind Angus's 'Escargot Écossais' is to address both these problems: he provides snails from his farm in every shape or form, including sauced and oven-ready, to retail outlets, restaurants and by post. And Angus has no intention of stopping there. He will not rest until the average consumer is stirring batches of his individual quick-frozen snails into seafood tagliatelle, coating them in a port and Stilton sauce and, more daring still, serving up snail terrine or smoked snails (marinaded on the farm then cooked slowly with herbs and spices over oak chips made from old whisky barrels) as the perfect dinner party starter. And, as he is quick to point out, since snails are low in fat and high in protein they are a perfect neutral 'protein-carrier' in any recipe.

So when you are next flicking through recipe books in search of inspiration, spare a thought for this young man in his 3000-sq ft snail shed with its controlled environment (18 hours of light, 8 hours of darkness), sterilising the soil, grading the growers, collecting the eggs – and all for the sake of the snail.

The following snail recipes are not strictly breakfast recipes but would make a deliciously different Sunday brunch. They were created by David McKendry, chef at the Taymouth Castle restaurant in Kenmore, Perthshire. These recipes call for IQF snails – individually quick-frozen (*see* Appendix). They should be defrosted before use (as you would for, say, prawns).

Snail Stir Fry
Serves 2

3–4 tablespoons hazelnut oil
120 g (4 oz) mange tout
1 red pepper, de-seeded and finely sliced

120 g (4 oz) baby corn
90 g (3 oz) pineapple, chopped; if tinned, drain well
2 garlic cloves, crushed
1 large carrot, finely sliced
1 onion, finely sliced
1 small mango, chopped
2.5 cm (1 in) piece fresh root ginger
soy sauce
Tabasco
salt and freshly-ground black pepper
1 doz IQF snails, defrosted

Sauté all the vegetables and pineapple in hazelnut oil, and season to taste with salt and pepper, soy sauce and Tabasco.

Add the snails, warm through for 2–5 minutes, and serve on a hot plate with rice or noodles. Garnish with asparagus tips (do not use tinned), Chinese spring onion curls and toasted pine kernels.

Snail Pâté
Enough for 2

4 shallots, finely chopped
120 g (4 oz) butter
120 ml (4 fl oz) crème fraîche
60 ml (2 fl oz) double cream
250 g (8 oz) IQF snails
Tabasco pepper sauce
Worcestershire sauce
a dash of malt whisky
salt and freshly-ground black pepper
salad leaves to garnish

Gently sweat the finely-chopped shallots in the butter. Add the crème fraîche and double cream, and reduce. Bring the sauce to the boil, add in the snails, then flavour with Tabasco, Worcestershire sauce and the whisky. Check the seasoning and consistency.

Liquidise the mixture in the blender. The final consistency should be 'dropping' (off the spoon). If it seems too thick, add a little more cream and another dash of whisky, and blend again. Spoon into two ramekin dishes, and leave to set. Later, seal with clarified butter.

Serve the pâté in the ramekins with oatcakes, garlic bread or melba toast. Redcurrant jelly is a delicious extra.

Snail Kebabs
For 4 kebabs, one per person

16 IQF snails, defrosted
1 red onion, cut in chunks
8 small mushrooms, halved
1 red pepper, de-seeded and cut into 8 pieces
1 courgette, thickly sliced

For the sauce

4 tablespoons double cream
120 ml (4 fl oz) crème fraîche
3 tablespoons coconut milk
salt and freshly-ground black pepper
1 tablespoon elderflower cordial (or 1 tablespoon of rum or liqueur, e.g. Glayvaar, Drambuie or Grand Marnier)

For the rice

> 250 g (8 oz) white long grain rice
> few strands saffron
> 1 tablespoon each fresh rosemary and coriander

Just cover the rice with boiling water and add a few strands of saffron. Cook for 15–20 minutes until the grains are separate and fluffy and most of the water has evaporated. Drain and keep warm.

Thread the kebab ingredients alternately onto skewers. Baste if desired with olive oil/white wine/lemon or lime juice. Grill for 8–10 minutes, turning often.

Meanwhile, gently heat the double cream and crème fraîche, stirring all the time, until reduced by half. Do not boil. Draw the pan off the heat and add the coconut milk. Return to the heat and cook for 1 minute, stirring. Remove the pan from the heat again and add lime juice and zest and elderflower cordial. Season.

Heat through the saffron rice, add the chopped fresh rosemary and coriander and serve with the kebabs and sauce. Garnish with more fresh herbs.

John and Jennie Makepeace

Near Beaminster, Dorset

It's not unknown for the breakfast host and hostess to go to a great deal of trouble for their 'On Your Farm' visitors, but few can have suffered the privations that Jennie Makepeace did in preparing her succulent scallops and bacon. Walking with her husband John, the furniture designer, at West Bay near Bridport a couple of days before the team was due to descend, they caught sight of the fishing fleet coming home. With breakfast menus uppermost in her mind, Jennie sped to the quay to see what the boats had on board. Finding enormous hessian sacks being loaded onto an articulated lorry and hearing that they were bound for the overnight ferry to France, she correctly assumed that they must contain something rare and delicious.

John opened the bargaining and the fishermen agreed to part with 'a few' for £3.50 – which was how Jennie came to spend the best part of the next day at the sink with a Stanley knife in her hand and a half-hundredweight sackful of 'queenies' – very tiny scallops – on the floor beside her. The day had its high points, like the whelks which had found their way into the sack and orienteered round the kitchen, but Jennie's hands took some punishment from the sharp knife and the small, tightly-closed shells. By the next day, however, she was on fine form again, using some of the 8½ lbs of scallop meat to produce a simple but memorable combination with some local bacon.

The resulting breakfast encapsulated on a plate Jennie's philosophy of food. She actively boycotts supermarkets, believing that if you live in a rural area you have a duty to support the local economy, buying locally-grown or -reared food from smaller shops or direct from the farms. Jennie supports her local baker, grocer and greengrocer where she supplements the produce from her own kitchen and herb garden. Though she and John do eat meat and fish (and her two sons will sometimes turn up for a 'meat feast' on a Sunday), Jennie is, she says, a 'closet vegetarian'.

Her family have always kept pigs and so did she until five years ago when she could no longer face the seeming betrayal of sending the animals (which practically followed her around) to the slaughterhouse. She keeps a flock of geese but any enquiries from hapless visitors along the lines of 'Do you eat your geese?' are met with a swift put-down: 'Would you eat your dog?' To which there is no answer.

Scallops and bacon
Serves 4

    8 rashers smoked back bacon
    3 scallops (or 6 'queenies') per person
    freshly-chopped parsley

Simply grill or fry the bacon, then keep warm.

Quickly turn the scallops in the bacon fat, tipped into a frying pan if the bacon has been grilled, and supplemented if necessary with a little vegetable oil. They will only take about 3 minutes to cook.

Place, sprinkled with chopped parsley, with the bacon on warmed plates. Serve with toast or (especially delicious) hot soda bread.

Adrianne and Tony Mills

Kitale, Kenya

Tony and Adrianne Mills were both born and brought up in Kenya and their 874-acre Lokitela Farm is at the foot of Mount Elgon in the heart of western Kenya's Trans-Nzoia district. As well as producing hybrid seed-maize and running a large dairy, Tony and Adrianne organise safaris from the farm and offer their guests traditional Kenyan farm hospitality. Guests can visit the Saiwa Swamp, Cherangani Hills and the dry country of West Pokot, but even the keenest birdwatchers could be tempted to wile away a few days at Lokitela itself where 300 varieties of birds have been recorded in the farm's own 70 acres of natural forest and garden.

Food is normally plentiful in Kenya which, though on the equator, rises to 6,000 feet. Breakfast at Lokitela is eaten at any time, depending on the farmwork the day will bring, but is always taken on the open verandah looking out towards Mount Elgon. Here, in caves, thousands of fruit-bats roost, clicking their tongues, while elephants gouge deep grooves in the volcanic rock with their tusks to extract the mineral salts they need to supplement their diet.

The tourist will need no such supplements – all the ingredients for a full 'English' breakfast are locally produced. But the staple diet of the locals is maize, known as *posho*. A true native breakfast would probably consist of a cup of sweetened tea or *ugi* – maize meal cooked with milk but made thin enough to drink. Local workers would eat only one main meal a day, again consisting of *posho* but cooked to a stiff mass so it can be picked up and eaten with the fingers. Vegetables – beans, okra, tomatoes or possibly carrots – with maybe a little meat or chicken would be the accompaniment.

Their numerous dogs, cats and Gilbert, the African parrot, often gather round on the verandah at 8.20 each morning which is when Adrianne or Tony makes radio contact with Nairobi. There is no phone at the farm and no electricity during the day but knowing and loving Kenya as they do, Adrianne and Tony feel that they already have more than they need.

Posho Porridge

Posho is ground maize meal and is the staple carbohydrate in many African countries. If maize meal is not available, corn meal (available in West Indian shops) could be an acceptable substitute: failing that, porridge oats will do! The addition of fruit turns *posho* porridge, which is very bland, into a rather more exciting start to the day.

3 heaped tablespoons *posho*/corn meal
3 cups milk (or water if preferred)
large pinch salt

Sieve the *posho* (or corn meal) into a saucepan with the milk or water. Bring to the boil, stirring continuously to stop lumps forming, until the mixture thickens which will take about 15 minutes. Serve with extra milk, sugar – and fruit.

Alternatively, make porridge with porridge oats in the usual way, using 3 level tablespoons (½ cup) and 1½ cups water, milk, or milk and water per person. Serve with Lokitela Fruit Dish given below, or any combination of fruits – excellent with red summer fruits and useful for using up fruit in glut.

Lokitela Fruit Dish

A selection from any of the following fruits, all of which are grown on the farm:

pawpaw, pineapple, bananas, mulberries, passion fruit, figs, loquats, cape gooseberries (better known now as Kiwi fruit), wineberries, strawberries, guavas, blackberries

Take a combination of fruits, depending on what is available at the time. Boil 150 ml (¼ pt) water with 1 tablespoon of brown sugar and pour over the mixed fruit. Leave to cool.

Mealie Pancakes

Another Kenyan speciality is made from green maize, also grown on the farm. The nearest British equivalent would be corn on the cob, and the following recipe could be made with drained, canned sweetcorn.

    4 eggs, separated
    240 g (8 oz) green maize (taken off the cob and
        minced)
    2 tablespoons plain flour
    pinch salt
    2 tablespoons sugar (brown if preferred)
    5 tablespoons cream and 5 tablespoons milk or 150
        ml (¼ pint) milk and a tablespoon of melted
        butter

Add beaten egg yolks to minced maize, then add flour, salt, sugar, milk or cream mixture and, finally, the well-beaten egg whites. Depending on the size of pancake required, drop mixture either from a dessertspoon or tablespoon onto a hot frying pan or griddle. Cook on both sides until brown. Serve with brown sugar mixed with cinnamon, or golden syrup, and/or thick farm cream.

John Nix and Sue Clement

Wye, Kent

John Nix is Emeritus Professor of Farm Business Management at Wye College, part of the University of London. The title makes him sound rather grand, possibly even stuffy. In fact, neither is the case. Nor would 'grand' and 'stuffy' be terms which could be applied to the breakfast which John and his partner, Sue Clement, served when 'On Your Farm' visited them in Kent; 'delicious' would be much nearer the mark. In fact, John recalls it as more like a scene from an Ealing comedy.

'The granola was something of a problem to prise from the jar,' he admits, 'and when we finally got some out, it was so sticky that Anthony Rosen had trouble in starting the conversation as his teeth were jammed together. Sue had also made some marmalade – for the first time – and that too was somewhat thick. I think we bent three spoons trying to extract it.' Sue is actually a very gifted cook and one with the courage to experiment: anyone who dares to try a couple of new recipes in front of a million listeners has got to know what they are doing. Her kedgeree was remembered by all who took part in the programme as 'sublime' and, fearless of her dentistry, the programme's producer, Carol Trewin, begged to be allowed to take some granola away with her as she thought it was so scrumptious. John and Sue swiftly pressed her to take the whole jar.

Crunchy Fruit Granola

Sticky but delicious!

For 12 portions
  5 tablespoons clear honey
  3 tablespoons soft light brown sugar
  340 g (12 oz) muesli cereal
  1 teaspoon lemon zest
  1 teaspoon real vanilla essence
  2 tablespoons sunflower or pumpkin seeds
  60 g (2 oz) nuts – hazelnuts are good; or walnuts or
    brazils or a mixture, very roughly chopped
  120 g (4 oz) dried apricots, chopped
  120 g (4 oz) dried apple, peach or pear rings, quar-
    tered

Heat the honey and brown sugar in a large, heavy saucepan over a low heat until the sugar has dissolved. Stir in the cereal, lemon, vanilla essence, and sunflower or pumpkin seeds and nuts. Turn the mixture onto two non-stick baking sheets and spread out evenly.

Bake in a pre-heated oven at 170°C/325°F/ Gas Mark 3 for 25 minutes, stirring around from time to time and then re-spreading on the baking sheets.

Remove from oven. Break up into a large bowl, add the dried fruit, stir and then leave to cool.

When cold, turn into a wide-necked airtight container – i.e. a tin or Tupperware but not a Kilner jar as this makes it too difficult to get the mixture out.

Serve with milk, thick yoghurt or fruit juice.

Kedgeree with Smoked Salmon

This is a brilliant recipe which can be prepared the day before and just needs finishing off before it is eaten.

Serves 8 for breakfast, 4 for supper
    225 g (8 oz) long-grain white rice
    ½ teaspoon turmeric
    225 g (8 oz) haddock fillet
    120 g (4 oz) butter
    120 g (4 oz) button mushrooms, sliced
    cayenne pepper
    2 tablespoons chopped parsley
    2 medium eggs – free range
    120 g (4 oz) smoked salmon – trimmings are fine
    salt and freshly-ground black pepper

optional garnish

    2 hard-boiled eggs, sliced
    extra parsley

Bring a large pan of salted water to the boil and add the rice and turmeric. Bring to the boil, then simmer for 12 minutes or until the rice still has a little 'bite' to it when tested. Drain well.

Cut the haddock into strips and fry in 30 g (1 oz) butter for about 5 minutes, or until just cooked. Remove from pan and keep warm.

Melt another 30 g (1 oz) butter and fry the mushrooms for about 2 minutes until they release their juices. Then mix together the drained rice, haddock and mushrooms. Leave to cool, then store, covered, in the fridge overnight.

Before serving, melt the remaining butter in a large pan and tip in the rice/fish/mushroom mixture. Heat gently, stirring but be careful not to break up the fish. Season well with black pepper and cayenne pepper, and stir in the two lightly beaten eggs and parsley.

Turn into a warmed serving dish and top with thin strips of smoked salmon. You can also add extra parsley or hard-boiled egg slices. Serve straightaway, on its own or with toast or granary rolls.

Anne Petch

Kings Nympton, Devon

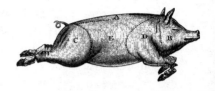

It all started with one lonely piglet, the runt of the litter, which had been rolled on by its mother. The farmer gave it to Anne Petch to raise on her family's smallholding and even when she was away at Art School, she would rush back at the weekends to keep an eye on her growing menagerie. This early experience turned Anne into a 'pig person' and she is fierce in defence of what she sees as a much maligned animal. Even amongst the Rare Breeds, she laments, pigs get a rough deal: the cattle, such as Longhorn, are immediately attractive whilst the sheep are easy to keep and cheap to feed. Neither applies to pigs – yet, she says, they are highly intelligent creatures which more than repay human devotion. Though she rears pigs, sheep and cattle at Heal Farm, there is no doubt that her first love has been her last.

Anne began meat production at Heal Farm twenty-five years ago. With great prescience, she began asking questions about the ingredients contained in animal foods and, unable to get straight answers, carried out her own investigations. Appalled at what she discovered about what she calls, tactfully, the 'inappropriate' ingredients contained in animal foodstuffs, Heal Farm immediately started having their rations mixed to their own recipe. Today, of course, her suspicions have been proved right but Anne displays as much sorrow as anger, and not a trace of smugness.

Her convictions, however, are stronger than ever. Clean, wholesome food for human consumption, she says, can only come as a result of natural, sustainable farming and she takes pride in having shaped attitudes towards responsible meat eating. Though she admits that turning her precious Rare Breed pigs into sausages and bacon may seem something of an irony, the logic is simple. Creating a supportive market for the meat means that more breeding animals will be kept and the future of the breeds secured. All Anne's animals are treated with care and respect and Anne speaks lyrically about the enjoyment they derive particularly when they are turned out to grass again after being housed inside all winter.

That Heal Farm is the holder of countless quality awards should come as no surprise: thousands of satisfied customers for Anne's mail-order meat, sausages and delicious recipe dishes are an even more eloquent testament to her success.

There are two important things about laver or laverbread, a type of seaweed which is a traditional Devon speciality. First, select it correctly. Laver (Latin names *Prophyra leucostica* or *Prophyra umbilicis*) is the soft, frondy seaweed which grows on rocks which are only exposed at low tide. It is a rich source of iron but traditionally, like oysters, it should only be eaten when there is an 'r' in the month. Do not make the mistake of gathering other types of seaweed, especially the common green seaweed which is bitter.

Secondly, wash it well by plunging it in bucket after bucket of cold water to make sure that all the sand is removed. Then cook slowly for several hours in dripping and a good sprinkling of vinegar, pepper and salt, or, even more simply, with a knob of butter. Like spinach, it boils down to almost nothing and turns a very very dark glossy green – almost black – in colour. Serve with toast, fried bread, eggs – and it is especially good with bacon.

If you are nervous about collecting it or do not live near the sea, it should be available from good fishmongers, already cooked, or you can even buy it tinned.

Anne Petch's Laverbread with Bacon
For 1 serving

4 tablespoons cooked laverbread
fine oatmeal to bind into a fairly firm mixture –
    about 2 to 3 tablespoons
bacon fat for frying

Mix the laverbread and oatmeal, form into little cakes and fry in bacon fat until the oatmeal is cooked and lightly browned. Serve immediately with bacon.

Variation
Make a light batter with 120 g (4 oz) flour, 1 large egg, just over 300 ml (½ pint) milk and a pinch of salt. Stir in 6 tablespoons of laverbread and cook in bacon fat as little pancakes.

85

Anne's Home-made Bangers
To make 32 sausages (see page 9)

960 g (2 lb) lean pork
480 g (1 lb) hard pork back fat
480 g (1 lb) fresh breadcrumbs
30 g (1 oz) salt
15 g (½ oz) ground white pepper
7 g (¼ oz) chopped fresh sage
good pinch each ground nutmeg and mace

Mince the meat and fat together coarsely, using a mincer or food processor, then mix in the other ingredients. You may of course fill your own hog casings in which case tie off in sausages weighing 90–120 g (3–4 oz) each; or you can ask your butcher very nicely if he would fill the cases for you – *see* page 22. The sausages can be either grilled or fried.

Peter and Jackie Petts

Prickwillow, Cambridgeshire

When Peter and Jackie Petts bought a house in 1985 with a 3-acre field attached, they were not in search of the good life so much as a paddock for a horse. With busy careers as communications consultants, they were also novice gardeners and the land which wasn't to be utilised as a pony paddock posed a problem. Peter pondered the situation. Both he and Jackie were frustrated with the fact that herbs which had been easily available fresh in the nearby deli in London were not in existence in the local shops – doubly so since the rich Fenland soil which surrounded them was so fertile. And there was a cunning ulterior motive: employing a horticultural college graduate to get the herbery started also let them off the gardening hook themselves.

Peter is the ideas man: Jackie has the follow-through which is necessary in a business which has now been established for ten years. Both are keen cooks, garnering inspiration and recipes from all over the world and not afraid to experiment either. Peter is probably the more enthusiastic, partly in rebellion against years of indifferent school food and partly in the belief that cookery is not some mystical process but something anyone can do. Like all good cooks, he has his trademark ingredients: the strong peppery taste of lovage has been a recent favourite, with savory a close second.

For the 'On Your Farm' breakfast, the Petts served food with a cosmopolitan flavour . . . and fresh herbs in abundance. The following were all served, and the ingredients are for four.

Bucks Fizz

> 1 bottle sparkling white wine or, if feeling flush,
>   Champagne
> 1 litre (1½ pints) freshly-squeezed orange juice

Serve very cold, mixed in equal parts.

Scrambled Eggs *aux Fines Herbes*

The herbs used here are the classic ingredient of *omelette aux fines herbes*; they are equally delicious with scrambled eggs.

> 6 fresh eggs
> 1 tablespoon milk
> salt and pepper

1 tablespoon of chopped fresh herbs, mixed:
  should include chives, tarragon, chervil and
  parsley
1 walnut-sized piece of butter
paprika

Whisk the eggs lightly with the milk and seasoning and fold in the chopped herbs. Have a warmed serving dish ready. Melt the butter in a saucepan, add the egg mixture and stir over a moderate heat until the egg begins to solidify. Take care not to overcook and turn the scrambled eggs into the serving dish just before they cease to be runny. (Left in the saucepan they will continue to cook.) Sprinkle with a little paprika and serve.

Grated Potato Pancakes with Tarragon

2 medium potatoes, coarsely grated
1 small onion, coarsely grated
1 generous pinch of freshly-chopped French tarragon
salt and pepper
oil for frying

Mix the grated potato, onion, tarragon and seasoning. Heat the oil in a large frying pan and spoon the mixture in, forming four flat cakes of equal size. Fry over a moderate heat, turning once, until cooked through, and crisp and brown on both sides.

Baked Tomatoes with Basil

 4 large, ripe tomatoes (preferably plum tomatoes)
 crystal sea salt or Maldon salt flakes
 black pepper
 fresh basil, roughly shredded

Remove the small core at the top of each tomato and slice downwards to halve them. Place the halves on a grill tray, sprinkle each with a little freshly-ground black pepper and a generous pinch of the salt crystals. Bake in a hot oven for 8 minutes and serve with the shredded basil on top.

Sausagemeat Balls with added Herbs

 250 g (½ lb) good quality sausages
 1 small onion, chopped very finely
 1 dessertspoon chopped and mixed parsley, thyme
   and savory
 freshly-ground black pepper
 parsley sprigs for garnish

Remove the sausage meat from the skins and mix the filling with the onion, herbs and black pepper. Mould the mixture with floured hands into 1½-in balls. Bake in a hot oven, or fry, for 15 minutes and serve garnished with parsley.

Mushrooms and Bacon with Chives

4 field mushrooms
1 teaspoon chopped chives
salt and freshly-ground black pepper
4 thick rashers of back bacon
chopped parsley to garnish

Remove and discard the stalks, then peel the mushrooms and place them cup upwards on a large sheet of cooking foil. Sprinkle chopped chives and seasoning into the cups. Cover each with a rasher of bacon, rind removed and cut into two parts to fit. Fold the foil and pinch the edges together to form an air-tight parcel. Place in a hot oven for 12 minutes. When cooked, open and serve the mushrooms, sprinkled with chopped parsley.

Francis and Maisie Pryor

Flag Fen, near Peterborough

Imagine a breakfast with no orange juice, no tea, no coffee, no eggs (incidentally, it took the Romans to introduce chickens to Britain). Instead, fetid cheese made with sheep's or cow's milk, a rather grainy porridge, and to drink, mead or beer. Still, there was always lunchtime to look forward to, with a choice of pork, sheepmeat, beef or horse, the chance of a duck or plover's egg, and salmon or caviar if by the sea. Such was the diet – in fact, rather more varied than one might have expected – in Bronze-Age Britain.

Archaeologists and sheep-keepers Francis and Maisie Pryor forbore to serve a Bronze Age breakfast when visited by 'On Your Farm', opting instead for a supremely civilised combination of scrambled eggs and asparagus, but in most other ways their lives are dedicated to this ancient period.

Excavations of the slub, or mud, at Flag Fen have revealed that agriculture at the time was more intensive than had previously been believed. Ditched fields were criss-crossed by droveways for their Soay sheep, a breed which had been established in Britain for well over a thousand years at the time of the Bronze Age, whose peak was at around 1000 BC, some 600 years after the building of Stonehenge. As a result, the people of the time were, on the whole, well nourished, as analysis of skeletons indicates, especially on the Fens where fishing provided a source of winter protein. The only conspicuous absence from the Bronze Age diet would seem to be vegetables, though the preponderence of fat hen, a weed often found in beet crops, suggests that it might have been cooked and served, though not, presumably, for breakfast.

Scrambled Eggs

The first rule, according to Francis whose speciality this is, is that scrambled eggs should be made in decent sized portions – at least two eggs per person, ideally two and a half. He does not add milk as he believes that this dilutes the result.

Per person
    2–2½ large eggs
    salt and freshly-ground black pepper
    1 large knob of unsalted butter

Break up the eggs lightly with a fork (not a whisk) and do not make them froth. If using unsalted butter, add a good sprinkling of sea salt and a generous grind of coarse black pepper. Heat the butter in a pan until liquid but not brown. Remove the pan from the heat and add the eggs. Return the pan to the heat (not a fierce flame: the cool plate of the Aga, or a low gas or half an electric ring), stirring lustily. Continue to stir while the eggs slowly heat until lumps just begin to form, snatching the pan entirely off the heat every twenty seconds or so.

Meanwhile, toast thick slices of bread (Francis favours white), butter generously and pour the eggs on top. Top with a grind of finely-ground green pepper (the secret ingredient). Serve quickly and enjoy!

Scrambled Eggs with Asparagus

The important point in this recipe is to make sure that the asparagus is cooked to perfection and does not dry up while the eggs cook. If you have a helping hand in the kitchen, then it should be quite easy to finish cooking the asparagus and eggs at the same time. It is difficult to give exact guidance because the size of the asparagus varies so much, but over-cooked asparagus is a dreadful waste . . .

Trim the spears generously as the thick base can be watery. This is a disaster when served with scrambled eggs as the toast absorbs the water and becomes a soggy mass. (Keep the thicker end of the stalks for soup.)

Steam the spears in an asparagus kettle until just *al dente*. Drain, then toss in butter which prevents them from going dry. Then immediately start to scramble the eggs, as indicated above. Amalgamate the eggs and toast, and serve with the asparagus – either laid beside the egg or over the top.

John and Mary Quicke

Newton St Cyres, Devon

It all goes back to war, explains John Quicke's daughter, Mary. It was then that it was decreed that the only cheeses made should be Cheddar and the seven or so 'territorials' like Cheshire and Leicester: the making of any other sort of cheeses was forbidden. After the war, there was such a demand for milk that there was none left over to recreate the half-forgotten English cheeses but now the news is good. Thanks both to farm diversification schemes and interest in healthier and more traditional ways of production, the number of British cheeses has climbed to a staggering 400.

The Quickes' interest in cheesemaking goes back to 1973 when Mary returned from an apprenticeship to a Cheshire cheesemaker to take over the production of traditional farmhouse Cheddar on the family's Devon farm. The process, as she describes it, is a genuine craft process, a true mixture of art and science: processing a 1,000-gallon vat of liquid milk into a solid calls on the senses of sight, smell, taste and touch as well as both the calmness and adaptability of mind to respond to changes in the cheese's texture which

95

might reveal a change in temperature or percentage of lactic acid.

The nearest comparison is probably winemaking and if there were such a thing for cheese, the Quickes' traditional, oak-smoked or herb Cheddar would be sure to qualify for an *appellation contrôlée*. The soft Credy valley climate, the rainfall and the soil which produce the rich pasture all contribute to a unique and highly localised taste, traceable back to the milk from their 400 Friesian–Holstein cross cattle. No wonder the result is described as having a 'long, full, rounded, nutty taste with a mature follow-through': rather than wine, it is, if anything, the Champagne of cheeses.

Cheese Dip

Delicious if rich on winter mornings, this is the breakfast with which the Quicke children were sent off to school.

Serves 4
   slice of butter
   120 g (4 oz) Quicke's mature Cheddar
   2 eggs
   splash of milk
   toast soldiers

Melt the butter in a pan over a low heat. Grate the cheese and mix with the eggs and milk. Add to the pan and stir until the eggs are beginning to set and the cheese is completely melted. Serve in ramekins or small dishes and dip in with toast soldiers.

Alternatively, spread the mixture on toast and

brown under the grill; it is especially delicious with grilled tomatoes.

It goes without saying that the herb or smoked Cheddar simply as cheese on toast is also delicious!

Cheese Dreams

For one
    2 slices wholemeal bread
    30 g (1 oz) butter
    60–90 g (2–3 oz) Quicke's mature Cheddar (to taste)

Make a cheese sandwich with the above ingredients, using about half the butter. Remove crusts and cut into triangles. Melt the remaining butter in a pan, and add the sandwiches. Fry briskly for a minute or so on each side until crisp. Drain on kitchen paper and serve immediately.

Cheesy Potatoes

Serves 4
    2 large left-over baked potatoes
    1 egg
    plenty of grated Quicke's mature Cheddar

Halve the potatoes. Carefully scoop out the insides, mix with beaten egg and plenty of cheese. Pile the mixture back into the hollow skins, sprinkle more cheese on top. Grill, or bake in a hot oven for 20–25 minutes. This is also delicious with herb or smoked Cheddar.

Peter and
Suzanne Redstone

Stokeinteignhead, Devon

The coldest breakfast he'd ever had, but the most delicious – that was Oliver Walston's verdict on the ice-
cream breakfast served to him when he visited Peter
and Suzanne Redstone on their dairy farm in Devon,
Middle Rocombe Farm. After a fruit starter – mango
sorbet – and before the coffee and cornflake ice cream,
Oliver sampled an ice cream 'full English breakfast' –
containing muesli, and sausage, egg and bacon. Not a
conventional breakfast, but then nothing is conventional about this couple, with their shared
American/English, marketing/artistic backgrounds.

Suzanne's fascination for ice cream goes way back
to her childhood holidays in New Hampshire: on
arrival in England in the seventies, she could not
believe what was sold here in the name of ice cream. In

1986 Suzanne and Peter finally realised a long-standing dream to offer American-style ice cream, made with the finest organic ingredients, to a British public when their first retail outlet opened in Torquay.

After eleven years, they are, if anything, even more excited by and about the product than when they began. In terms which Peter's ex-management consultant colleagues would understand, their 'mission statement' is simple: ice cream is a food and deserves the same respect given to any other gourmet food. Since they started, the Redstones have created over 2,200 flavours. Are there any new challenges left? Yes, says Peter – to take old-established favourites and make them even better. Like the chocolate ice cream with chips of Malteser. Like the home-made honeycomb mingled with caramel and vanilla ice cream. Like the Drambuie chocolate truffle . . . Cornet, anyone?

Coffee Cornflake Ice Cream

This quantity will make 1–1½ litres of ice cream (depending on your machine – and an ice cream maker is essential for this recipe).

720 ml (24 fl oz) whipping cream
240 ml (8 fl oz) full cream milk
150 g (5 oz) raw cane sugar
3–4 free range eggs, depending on size
2 tablespoons good freeze-dried coffee
½ cup of fresh, crisp, uncrushed cornflakes

Heat the cream, milk and sugar in a heavy-bottomed saucepan. Stir until the sugar is dissolved and the mixture hot but not boiling.

Whisk the eggs in a bowl and slowly pour in approx. 240 g (8 oz) of the cream mix. Whisk until smooth then pour back into the rest of the mix in the saucepan. Whisk over a low heat until the mixture thickens slightly, and coats the back of a spoon. It is important that the mixture does not boil. Draw your finger across the back of the coated spoon: if the line remains, the ice cream base is ready.

Add the coffee and, if desired, extra sugar (to taste). Whisk over a warm heat until well blended.

Cool and then freeze in an ice-cream maker, according to manufacturer's instructions. Just before the ice cream is set, after it stiffens, stir in the cornflakes. Then put in the freezer to harden.

Soften the ice cream slightly before eating. If you like a slightly crunchier version, the cornflakes can be stirred in right at the end.

Miriam Rothschild

Ashton Wold, Northamptonshire

It's hard to know where to begin with Miriam Rothschild: her list of credits is endless – as a botanist, zoologist, entymologist and conservationist. She is also one of the world's leading experts on fleas – she was the person who spotted the link between fleas and myxomatosis and became the Government's adviser on the subject. In her younger days (she is now aged nearly ninety) she was a notable horsewoman and sportswoman, playing squash rackets and cricket for England. Her formal education at the hands of a governess whom she remembers only as 'rather fat' may have ended at the Romans but clearly the mental energy she did not have to expend on multiplication tables and the rules of grammar was far better employed in informing herself on every subject under the sun.

Ashton, near Peterborough, where she lives, is an estate village with that preserved-in-aspic look of an AA gazetteer of the 1930s. Thatched roofs top cottages built of local stone, but the village is not merely quaint.

The Rothschilds, the banking family who built it, were enlightened landlords – this was the first village in England where every house had a bathroom. Miriam Rothschild's own house, swathed in ivy, is long and low. The creeper teems with birds, insect and animal life: Miriam welcomes all comers, including the rats who nest among the slippery green leaves.

At the back of the house, high double doors lead into a garden which progresses through lawns where slender iris and variegated tulips push up through the grass to what Miriam calls a 'mini-meadow', vibrant in May with a sight you will not see anywhere else in England – thousands upon thousands of cowslips. The wild flowers in turn attract insects and butterflies (another passion) and the non-intensive farming practised at Ashton means that it literally teems with wildlife, to her unceasing delight.

Her views on food are irrevocably linked with her views on animal welfare. In her book *Animals and Man*, she declared that anyone who visited a slaughterhouse would instantly become, as she is, a vegetarian. Her disgust at the stress suffered by animals both at the abattoir and what she calls their 'sad and uncomfortable' journey to it caused her to give up keeping cattle, but she still keeps chickens which enjoy, she says 'an agreeable life' on the farm. She makes a point of eating the whites of two hens' eggs every day, avoiding the yolks because of the cholesterol they contain. (She does, though, allow herself the yolks of the smaller quail's egg.)

Miriam Rothschild's vegetarianism extends to a refusal to wear leather shoes: she habitually wears wellingtons, whether gardening, reading, or attending a Buckingham Palace party. Her beautiful house is a retreat for writers, musicians and painters – and, above all, friends. Books, flowers, teacups and plates of cake cover every surface. Charming, hospitable and enthusiastic, she rules her kingdom like a benign Circe.

Egg Pancakes

Serves 2–4 people, depending on appetite and how you make the pancakes

2 large potatoes, peeled and cut into chunks
salt, pepper, mint
oil and bacon fat
4 eggs
1 tablespoon cream

Boil the potatoes with a little salt, black pepper and mint. When cooked, mash the potatoes but do not add butter or milk.

Put a little oil into a frying pan, enough to coat the bottom of the pan. Place several spoonfuls of the mashed potato in the pan, pressing down to form a sort of pancake, and cook until golden brown on one side only. This amount of mixture will make two thin pancakes: if you prefer, you can use the mixture at one time to make one thick pancake. Slide the pancake onto a serving plate, uncooked side up, and keep warm.

Fry the eggs in bacon fat and, when cooked enough so that the yolks are just firm, transfer to a plate or bowl, chop and bind with the cream. For two pancakes: spoon the mixture onto one half, fold over the other half and serve. For one thick pancake: place the mixture on top of the pancake and serve cut in wedges.

Elderflower Cordial

There is no great mystique about gathering elder-flower heads. Obviously do not pick them from the roadside: they will have absorbed too much pollution. The elderflower heads must be cut off immediately below the main stalk, and afterwards the fine stalks leading to the flowers should also be removed. The best moment to collect these heads is when the flowers have just opened – buds are not suitable and avoid brownish flowers which are past their best. Provided you have chosen your picking place carefully, it should not be necessary to wash the elderflower heads. Simply shake them to dislodge any insect life; any you miss will be caught in the muslin when the mixture is strained.

30 heads of elderflower
2 kg (4 lb) granulated sugar
2 sliced lemons
75 g (2½ oz) citric acid

Put all the ingredients into a sterilised white bucket. Pour on 1.5 litres (2½ pints) of boiling water, and place in an *inconvenient* place so you remember to stir it every morning and every evening for 5 days.

Strain the liquid through muslin, and then pour into sterilised screw-top bottles. Dilute to taste.

Lord and Lady Selborne

Selborne, Hampshire

One would have to be something of a philistine to live in Selborne, practically in the shadow of the Gilbert White museum and the church where he is buried, and not take account of the natural world. The great eighteenth-century writer and naturalist, returning today, might find much to alarm him and much which he would criticise in the changes to his beloved countryside, but none of them would he find at Temple Manor.

Lord and Lady Selborne's commercial orchards grow a huge variety of fruit on a massive scale, but it is in their garden where the retiring reverend would feel most at home. There, he could rest his back against a tree trunk which might be any one of seventy varieties of apples and pears, and watch the tits and finches at work and at play. Rousing himself for a stroll, he would observe quinces, medlars, mulberries, black, red and white currants, gooseberries, rhubarb and a well-tended vegetable garden.

Lingering by the kitchen door, and depending on the time of year, he might smell a waft of blackcurrant jam, quince jelly, or the tang of bitter marmalade, since Joanna Selborne is an accomplished cook with an enviable collection of apple, pear, quince and soft fruit recipes. She favours simple, unfussy cooking to bring out the flavour of good-quality ingredients, using fresh produce from the farm and garden wherever possible. These can include pheasant, wild duck and culled venison. The fish for the Selbornes' breakfast fish cakes came from a little further afield. This did nothing to diminish how delicious they were.

Fish Cakes
Makes 8 fish cakes

    480 g (1 lb) haddock or cod
    480 g (1 lb) potatoes
    good knob of butter
    salt and freshly-milled black pepper
    lemon juice
    2 tablespoons fresh parsley, finely chopped
    2 small eggs, beaten
    toasted breadcrumbs
    oil, for frying

Just cover the fish with water and simmer with the parsley stalks for 7 minutes. Remove the skin and flake the fish.

Cook the potatoes until soft and mash with the butter. Add salt and pepper and lemon juice to taste. Add the flaked fish and parsley, shape into cakes. Dip these first in beaten egg, then breadcrumbs. Fry in hot oil for a few minutes on both sides or brush a baking tray with oil and bake in a hot oven until brown and crisp.

Hugo and Helen Sprinz

Beverley, East Riding of Yorkshire

The hired farmhands of the nineteenth century set more store by the food supplied on the farm than their wages: in Yorkshire, word went round at the hiring fairs of a 'good meat house' where beef or mutton would have been on the menu three times a day. And not without reason: the working day began at 5 a.m., readying the horses for ploughing, and was broken by breakfast at eight, lunch at twelve and tea at five and, depending on the season, was followed by more work on the land or in the stable. Regular supplies of carbo-hydrate and protein were essential.

This goes some way to explaining the breakfast spread which was laid on by Hugo and Helen Sprinz of Beverley in the East Riding: cold roast beef, home-made bread, pickles and cheese. But there was another unusual accompaniment which is also a Yorkshire tra-dition: apple pie, cooked on a flat plate and served as part of the morning meal. Tradition even extends as far as the way the pie must be cut. Each person at the table was asked to help him or herself by placing two fingers on the pie to anchor it and cutting the size of slice desired on either side. This method satisfied two basic requirements of hygiene and hospitality: no one else's piece of pie would be touched and each person could take the portion he desired.

Helen's Apple Pie

960 g (2 lb) Bramley apples
480 g (1 lb) self-raising flour
pinch of salt
60 g (2 oz) caster sugar
240 g (½ lb) of cooking margarine
2 eggs

First peel and core the apples and cook in as little water as possible. Sweeten to taste with a little extra sugar and leave to cool.

Mix the flour, salt and sugar in a bowl. Rub in margarine until the mixture resembles fine crumbs. Add the eggs and a little cold water to mix. Knead into a ball and leave to rest in a cool place/fridge for ½ hour.

Roll out the pastry and use to line a 25-cm (10-inch) pie plate, keeping some back for the lid. Add the cooked apples and a vented pastry lid. Cook at 180°C/350°F/Gas Mark 4 for approx. 45 minutes. If the pie browns too quickly, cover with foil or grease-proof paper to ensure that the bottom is fully cooked. It may be eaten hot, warm or cold.

Captain Bill Swinley

Flaxley, Gloucestershire

'Passions fired by widowed farmer's burnt breakfast' read the headline in the *Daily Telegraph* following the programme featuring Captain Bill Swinley. It referred to Bill's spectacular hopelessness in the kitchen which had resulted in his burning the crêpes (a Forest of Dean variant on Crêpes Suzette) which he had been planning to serve, and the resultant avalanche of letters and telephone calls from ladies anxious to look after him.

Bill freely admits that he is 'a terrible cook' but having spent a large part of his life eating 'matron's leg' (jam roly-poly – at boarding school) and 'baby's head' (tinned steak and kidney pudding – beneath the waves as a submariner), it is hardly surprising that his attitude to food and cooking is somewhat cavalier. Long months at sea, with its extraordinary diet (a favourite on 'midget' submarines was 'pot mess', the contents of six or seven random tins of whatever came to hand, boiled up together in a carpenter's glue pot) were punctuated by stops in exotic locations and a lengthy sojourn in the Bahamas with its glorious tropical fruits. (Indeed, another casualty of the breakfast was presenter Quentin Seddon's dental work when he nearly broke a tooth on the stone in a Jamaican tamarind ball.) The beer bread was almost as much of a challenge – Bill had to apologise for being indistinct at one point as it had jammed his teeth together.

The only disappointment, given that it was Christmas time and that Bill farms twenty-three varieties of plums, was that there was no plum pudding on the table. Bill, however, can justify its omission: the 'plum' in plum pudding, he says, refers not to the ingredients but to the old-fashioned method of cooking a Christmas pudding which was to wrap it in a cloth and hang it over a steaming pot of water on the range by suspending it from a tripod using a *plumb line*.

Christmas pudding Swinley-style has, however, traditionally contained plums as opposed to Bill's despised inferior foreign fruits such as currants and sultanas. He is the first to admit, however, that it is a confection way beyond his culinary abilities. These days, he specialises in heating up food his daughter-in-law has cooked and placed in the freezer, and in making plum wine – what he can't drink is, according to him, 'an excellent weedkiller'. It would be nice to think he was joking – but with Bill, you never quite know.

29/9. Did with ½ quantity of sugar + Guiness + salt. Omit sugar next time. The Guiness could be tasted and the dough was a kind of wholemeal colour. Try l...

Bill Swinley's Beer Bread

This recipe was given to Bill by an American in the Bahamas. It needs no yeast: the yeast in the beer does all the work.*

- 1 can of beer (to taste but Newcastle Brown Ale is a good bet)
- 2 tablespoons granulated sugar
- 480 g (1 lb) self-raising flour

Bill says:
Put it all together in a large bowl and stir it around a bit until you get a dough. Add a bit more flour or beer depending on how it looks. Sling it in a buttered pan and put it in the oven until it rises and looks cooked.

or, more conservatively interpreted
Mix all ingredients together in a large bowl until the right consistency is achieved, adding more flour or liquid as necessary to achieve a pliable dough. Place in a greased 500-g (1-lb) loaf tin and cook at 230°C/450°F/Gas Mark 8 for 25–30 minutes. The bottom should sound hollow when tapped.

* This is nonsense, for canned beer contains no live yeast, and even if it did the oven heat would kill it before it could do its stuff. But the method does work so I think that what happens is that the CO_2 dissolved in the beer makes the dough rise by aerating it.

111

Julian and Diana Temperley

Kingsbury, Somerset

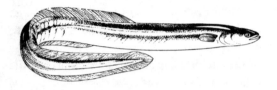

There has been cider made on Julian Temperley's Somerset farm for at least 150 years and though he grew up there he still maintains that, like everyone else in the business, he fell into cider making by mistake. Over the years, he has raised cider making to an art form and is single-handedly responsible for the re-creation of English Cider Brandy, a product which was first distilled in this country in 1678. Whilst his Burrow Hill cider sells plentifully locally, the cider brandy can be found in Germany and Japan as well as in specialist retailers and supermarkets in this country.

Julian is a passionate ambassador for apples in general and Somerset apples in particular, which, thanks to the soil and climate, are unique and, he says, world class. Constantly asked why he was not producing Calvados, he set out to create a product which did not ape its French counterpart (or 'cousin' as he likes to think of it) but would reflect the character of the

Somerset apple. The resulting cider brandy he describes as 'longer, softer and lighter' than Calvados, and with a more apply taste.

Julian has never had any trouble from the French over the similarity of the product: he admits that he has borrowed their maturing techniques but always knew the products would taste different because the apples are different. To expect them to taste the same would, he says, be to expect a Burgundy to taste like a Bordeaux. The French have taken the attitude that cider brandy can only expand rather than threaten the Calvados market, and this has proved to be the case.

Julian is proud of being an artisan/producer in the Continental style (he uses no concentrates), but he is determined not to die on the stake of a museum activity and, in fact, the Somerset Cider Brandy Company – owned by several Somerset cider makers – is the only commercial distiller and the biggest producer of cider brandy in Europe. As part of a long and distinguished tradition, Julian is intent on producing a legitimate product which has found its niche in the English drinks market for years to come.

Smoked Eel and Scrambled Eggs

Eel – if not smoked eel – is a traditional Somerset delicacy. According to the Domesday Book, local monks were allowed to receive 1,400 eels a year from local fishermen out of a total production of 5,000. The flesh is firm and succulent, slightly sweet with a delicate flavour. *See* the Appendix for a recommended stockist.

per person

Lightly beat two eggs and a little milk or cream, adding salt and pepper. Heat butter until foaming in a heavy-based pan and add the eggs, stirring constantly, but do not allow them to overcook and become dry – they are best served slightly runny. Slice the smoked eel. Scatter slices of smoked eel on top for a real Somerset breakfast.

Hillary and Michael Thompson

Blairgowrie, Perthshire

Buried among the buttercups, the stone farmhouse at Blairgowrie looks like the perfect rural idyll. When you hear that Hillary is an artist and Michael is involved in marketing, you might for a moment think them incomers who have retreated to the countryside from the fleshpots of Edinburgh. Far from it. Both are busy working farmers. The farm is the base for Michael's work with Scottish Soft Fruit Growers Limited – a producer organisation dedicated to getting the best deal for local growers in a surprisingly volatile market.

While Michael is busy marketing, Hillary runs 120 acres of permanent set-aside, plus rotational set-aside, rape and, of course, the raspberries for which Tayside is famous. She also makes the most sensational raspberry jam which 'cooks' in the freezer rather than on top of the stove.

Hillary freely admits that whilst she is a fair cook she is not a jam maker, which is why she seized avidly on the no-cook recipe when it was offered by a friend's mother. The advantage of the no-cook method is to retain the full flavour of the fruit, giving a fresher taste than in a boiled jam – actually, it is more a fruit purée than anything else. The resultant ruby-coloured mixture is also perfect for filling cakes and pancakes, using in trifles, and so on. Guests and visitors are always treated to a raspberry pudding at Blairgowrie, although Hillary's own preference is simply to eat the fruit fresh, with cream. And, heretical as it sounds, don't expect Michael to ask for seconds – or even firsts – of anything containing raspberries. After a lifetime of growing them he is immune to their charms. For him, at breakfast, it has to be marmalade!

Hillary Thompson's Freezer Raspberry Jam

  1 kg (2¼ lb) raspberries
  1.8 kg (4 lb) caster sugar
  4 tablespoons lemon juice
  1 bottle 'Certo' pectin

In a large bowl, crush the berries. Add the sugar and leave for 1 hour, stirring occasionally. Add the lemon juice and 'Certo' and stir for 2 minutes. Pour into containers – margarine or butter tubs will do – but do leave ½ inch of headroom. Cover with foil. Leave in the kitchen for 48 hours before placing them in the freezer.

Defrost as required at room temperature. Once defrosted, the jam keeps well in the fridge.

Mike and Julie Turner

Bideford, Devon

Julie Turner's introduction to cheesemaking couldn't have been more graphic: when she was a child and the July skies turned low and thundery, the unpasteurised milk on her family's Devon dairy farm turned solid rather than sour. Her mother hung up the resulting lumps in muslin cloths and let them drip. Julie and her siblings enjoyed the heavenly, creamy, curd cheese which resulted, especially when spread thickly on home-baked bread – sometimes with salt and freshly snipped chives but more often sprinkled with sugar.

Now, Julie laments, the onset of pasteurised everything makes the process much harder but does not affect the yogurt which she makes and which she served Robert Forster when he breakfasted with Julie and her husband Mike at their sheep enterprise in north Devon.

Necessity became the mother of invention for the Turners when the link road to the M5 motorway literally cut the farm in half. Putting yogurt and cheese-making to one side for an evening, the family sat around the kitchen table for a brainstorming session. Someone came up with the novel idea of sheep races to pull in the visitors whose coaches and cars were whizzing past the farm.

Thus 'The Big Sheep' was born in 1988. It now offers anything and everything to do with sheep. The Turners have contrived to get their sheep lambing pretty well all year round so visitors can bottle-feed lambs, and in fine weather watch sheep-shearing and wool spinning or sheepdog demonstrations – as well as those infamous sheep races. The business has gone from strength to strength, now employing fifty people at the height of the season.

Julie describes herself as 'a typical Devonian farmer's wife – mean'. What she means is that she is loathe to spend money on food when there is such an abundance of it in the countryside for free. She wouldn't dream of visiting a greengrocer when there are blackberries in the hedgerows and mushrooms in the autumn fields, and every winter her family goes beachcombing for laver which, cooked slowly in beef dripping with vinegar and seasoning, turns to a dark, iron-rich mass, perfect to eat with fried bread or toast. (*See* page 85 for washing instructions.)

The teashop at The Big Sheep also benefits from Julie's farmhouse upbringing and offers such delicacies as Auntie Tish's Toenail Cake (for the faint-hearted better described as a rich sort of flapjack). Julie may describe herself as a typical Devonian but her positive outlook and entrepreneurial streak have shades of the transatlantic management guru. Her food, however, remains strictly close to home.

Sheep's Milk Yogurt

This can also be made with cow's milk although this produces a runnier result. To counteract this, stir in a couple of teaspoons of dried milk powder.

The first essentials for yogurt are scrupulously clean utensils. As well as being a basic hygiene concern, this is crucial in yogurt-making as the only bacteria which is to be encouraged is that which will make the yogurt culture. The first step, then, is to sterilise the bowl, spoon and strainer which will be used.

Having done this, boil a pint or more of milk. With sheep's milk, a microwave is perfect for this: as it is so rich it tends to stick to the sides of a saucepan. Having boiled it, cool to 42°C (blood temperature), using a jam thermometer to ascertain temperature. Put a teaspoon of any natural yogurt (live or dead) in the bottom of the clean bowl and pour on the warm milk, stirring all the time. Cover it with clingfilm and place inside a larger bowl or pan in case of spillage. Julie finds that the front left-hand side of the Aga is the perfect place to keep her yogurt warm for the necessary 4 hours, but any warm place will do, e.g. airing cupboard, warmed sterilised vacuum flask.

After 4 hours, the yogurt is ready to eat. You may prefer to chill it first. It is delicious plain, or with additions such as fresh fruit, muesli, raspberry jam, etc.

Guy and Sheila Woodall

Alresford, Hampshire

If Guy or Sheila Woodall had ever appeared on 'Mastermind', they would have had no problem in choosing a suitably baffling specialised subject: it would have to have been 'small ales'. This young couple have become authorities on the subject as a result of old family recipes which were passed down and which they had the foresight not just to make for themselves but for a wider and highly appreciative audience. Less appreciative were the French Champagne houses who took the Woodalls to court to try to stop them referring to their sparkling elderflower drink as 'champagne'. (The Champagne houses won.)

Before the invention of modern carbonated drinks, 'small ales' were the popular way of quenching a thirst. They were infusions of common plants – 'Let's be frank, weeds,' interjects Guy – which were lightly fermented to give them what he describes as 'a fresh flavour – and, if fermented in a sealed bottle, a lively sparkle'. They could contain up to about 1½ per cent alcohol but were effectively considered 'soft drinks' and hence looked down on by the liquor-drinking classes. Their twin appeal lay in their fresh flavour as well as the supposedly beneficial properties of the plants used.

In reproducing the drinks for a modern market, however, Guy and Sheila have had to make some adjustments. Older recipes called for lengthy boiling of the ingredients: Guy prefers a process of osmotic extraction or simple maceration which, he believes, preserves more of the herbs' inherent goodness. The following two versions of the same Nettle Ale are thus separated by a generation or two of know-how – and Guy's keen appreciation of the modern, cleaner, palate.

Nettle Beer (Old recipe)

'The Nettle Beer made by cottagers is often given to their old folk as a remedy for gouty and rheumatic pains, but apart from this purpose it forms a pleasant drink at any time of the day. It may be made as follows:

'Take 2 gallons of cold water and a good pailful of washed young Nettle tops, add 2 or 3 large handfuls of Dandelion, the same of Clivers (Goosegrass) and 2 oz of bruised, whole ginger root. Boil gently for 40 minutes, then strain and stir in 2 teacupfuls of brown sugar. When lukewarm, place on the top a slice of toasted bread, spread with 1 oz of compressed yeast, stirred until liquid with 1 teaspoon of sugar. Keep it warm for 6 or 7 hours, then remove the scum and stir in 1 tablespoonful of cream of tartar. Bottle and tie the corks securely. The result is a specially wholesome sort of Ginger Beer.

'The juice of 2 lemons may be substituted for Dandelions and Clivers. Other Herbs are often added to Nettles in the making of Herb Beer, such as Burdock, Meadowsweet, Avens Horehound, the combination making a refreshing summer drink.'

Nettle Beer (Guy's 20th-century method)

Pailful washed nettle tops
3–4 large handfuls each of dandelion and clivers
   (goosegrass)
juice of 2 lemons
2 teacupsful light soft brown sugar
1 oz yeast (any sort)
1 tablespoonful cream of tartar
2 gallons water

Take your washed nettle tops and, without adding any further water, put them in a saucepan with a tight lid on a hot stove. At this point, add any other green herbs you propose to use if they are of the type which needs to be wilted in order to give up their flavour. As soon as the leaves are showing signs of beginning to wilt, after about 1 minute, remove the pan from the heat and stir in the brown sugar. (The ginger is omitted from Guy's method as he finds it fights with the subtle flavours of the herbs.) Add the cream of tartar, and any fresh herbs which do not need wilting, such as meadowsweet or elder flowerheads.

Leave to stand in a cool place for about 2 days, during which time the sugar will draw the flavour from the herbs, before adding the water, lemon juice and some yeast. Let this mixture stand at room temperature until you see the first signs of tiny bubbles appearing on the surface, indicating that the yeast has started to work.

Strain the liquor off into strong bottles: ordinary lemonade bottles are *not* strong enough to hold the pressure and dangerous explosions can result. Smaller bottles can take higher pressures, so beer bottles with crown corks are good, and Champagne bottles are ideal.

Leave for 2–3 weeks until the fermentation is over and the liquid has fallen bright. The only problem now is how to drink it avoiding the yeast, which tends to get roused up as soon as you open the bottles. If you can't put up with this, you can buy plastic Champagne-type stoppers with valves in. Store the bottles upside down so that the yeast settles on the stopper and, before opening, let the yeast out through the valve.

Appendix

Leo and Sarah Barclay

Rannoch Smokery
Kinloch Rannoch
by Pitlochry
Perthshire
PH16 5QD
Tel: 01882 632344
Fax: 01882 632441

Goods available by mail order or in person: opening hours Mon–Fri 9.00–5.00.

Sandy and Jayne Boyd

Chatsworth Farm Shop
Stud Farm
Pilsley
Bakewell
Derbyshire
DE45 1UF
Tel: 01246 583392
Fax: 01246 582514

Opening times; Mon–Sat 9.00–5.00, Sunday 11.00–5.00. Mail order also available: please write or telephone for details.

Helen Browning

Eastbrook Farm Organic Meats
Bishopstone
Swindon
Wiltshire
SN6 8PW
Tel: 01793 790460
Fax: 01793 791239

This is the address for fresh meat, home delivery nationwide in the UK. There is also a shop for personal customers:

Eastbrook Farm Shop
50 High Street
Shrivenham
Wiltshire
SN6 8AA
Tel: 01793 782211

Open Mon–Fri 8.00–5.30. Sat 8.00–1.30.

Dougal Campbell

For Pencarrig or Tyn Gryg cheeses please contact
Marilyn Jones.
Tel: 01570 422772
Mon–Fri 9.00–5.00.

Kenneth and Carla Carlisle

Wyken Vineyard and the Leaping Hare Café and
Country Store
Stanton
Bury St Edmunds
Suffolk
IP31 2DW
Tel: 01359 250287

Vineyard open to the public all the year round except
the month of January, on Thursdays, Fridays and
Sundays from 10.00–6.00. Also on Saturdays in the
months of November and December. Groups can visit
by appointment on Wednesdays.

Mail order wine sales can be arranged: telephone for a
list.

The Leaping Hare Café is open Thursdays, Fridays
and Sundays 10.00–6.00 and also on Friday evenings.

Nick and Sheila Charrington

Layer Marney Tower
Layer Marney
Near Colchester
Essex
CO5 9US
Tel and Fax: 01206 330784

House/tearoom open from Easter until first Sunday
in October, every day except Saturday, from 12.00–
5.00.

Winter months: shop open Mon–Fri 9.00–5.00. (Ring doorbell for service!)

John and Christian Curtis

Easter Weens
Bonchester Bridge
Hawick
Roxburghshire
TD9 8JQ
Tel and Fax: 01450 860635

Gave up in 1998 because of govt. persecution

They do not do mail order but will sell cheese 'at the back door' to callers. Their cheeses are available through Neal's Yard Dairy (0171 379 7646) and are also sold by Ian Mellis in Edinburgh (0131 226 6215).

John and Nichola Fletcher

Reediehill Deer Farm
Auchtermuchty
Fife
KY14 7HS
Tel: 01337 828369
(For those with new style phones dial 07000 VENISON)
Fax: 01337 827001

Open 7 days a week 8.00–7.00.

Mail order: overnight home delivery service of fresh venison and products is also available throughout the UK, please write or telephone for a list.

Alan and Jackie Gear

Henry Doubleday Research Organisation
Ryton Organic Gardens
Coventry
CV8 3LG
Tel: 01203 303517
Fax: 01203 639229

Opening hours: gardens, shop and tearoom: Mon–Sun 10.00–5.00.

Sue and Michael Gibson

Edinvale Farms
Dallas
Moray
IV36 0RW
Tel: 01343 890265
Fax: 01343 890404

Ring for mail order brochure – beef/lamb/pork/game delivered overnight anywhere in the UK.

Shop:
Macbeth's Meats
11 Tolbooth St
Forres
Moray
IV36 0DB
Tel: 01309 672254.
Opening times: Mon–Sat 9.00–5.00.

Henry Head

Norfolk Lavender Ltd
Caley Mill
Heacham
Norfolk
PE31 7JE
Tel: 01485 570384
Fax: 01485 571176

Farm, shop and tearoom open May–September 9.00–5.30. Open over the winter but advisable to check ahead for exact times.

Mail order service available: Telephone 01485 572383 for catalogue.

Natalie Hodgson

Astley Abbotts House
Bridgnorth
Shropshire
WV16 4SW
Tel: 01746 763122

The house is open from 10.00–6.00 every day from mid-July to the end of August for Pick-Your-Own lavender, lavender bags, essential oils and lavender plants. The shop also sells honey and beeswax.

Patrick Holden

The Soil Association
86 Colston Street
Bristol
BS1 5BB
Tel: 0117 929 0661

Write or telephone (open Mon–Fri 9.30–5.30) for advice, or information about where and how to acquire organic produce.

Andrew Lane and John Noble

Loch Fyne Oysters Limited
Clachan Farm
Cairndow
Argyllshire
PA26 8BH
Tel: 01499 600264

The shop is open: winter 9.00–5.00, summer 9.00–8.00 or 9.00, seven days a week. Mail order also available.

Hugh Lillingstone

Innes Co.
Highfields
Statfold
Near Tamworth
Staffordshire
B79 0AQ

Tel: 01827 830197
Fax: 01827 830628

There are plans during 1997 to welcome visitors to the farm. Please telephone ahead for details, also for product list of sour-dough bread and Hugh's curd cheeses.

Angus Maxwell Macdonald

Gortinanane Snail Farm
Tayinloan
Argyllshire
P29 6XG
Tel: 01583 441331

There are plans during 1997 to open the farm, the largest in the UK and the only one in Scotland, to the public. Please telephone for details. Escargot Écossais can send IQF snails and cook-chilled snail dishes by post in poly boxes to any part of the UK. Please telephone for further details.

John and Jennie Makepeace

Parnham House
Near Beaminster
Dorset

Parnham House is open to the public from Easter until the end of October on Tuesdays, Wednesdays, Thursdays and Sundays from 10.00–5.00.

Adrianne and Tony Mills

Lokitela Farm
Kitale
Kenya

You can contact Tony Mills Safaris at PO Box 122, Kitale, Kenya, or fax to 00 254 325 20695.

Anne Petch

Heal Farm Meats
Kings Nympton
Umberleigh
Devon
EX37 9TB
Tel: 01769 574341
Fax: 01769 572839

Mail order meats and country foods – beef, pork, lamb, ham and bacon, sausages and burgers, recipe dishes, delicatessen and country foods.

Mouthwatering brochure, they even do a dinner party 'kit' – raw materials for 6 for £60, inc delivery.

Visitors to the farm shop are also welcome.
Open Mon–Fri 9.00–5.00.
Saturday 10.00–4.00.
Closed Sundays and Bank Holidays.

Peter and Jackie Petts

The Herbary
Prickwillow
Ely
Cambridgeshire
CB7 4SJ

Mail order only. Telephone for details on 01353 688456.

Francis and Maisie Pryor

Flag Fen
Fengate
Peterborough
Tel: 01733 313414

Open to the p ublic seven days a week, all year round except Christmas Day and Boxing Day from 11.00–5.00 (last admissions 3.30). There is an admission charge.

Winter months: 35 minute video and signposted trail of the site, which includes a Museum of the Bronze Age. The archaeological dig is closed over the winter for fear of frost damage but guided tours of the dig itself are available after the end of March until September/October.

There is also a coffee shop, gift shop and bookshop.

John and Mary Quicke

Quicke's Cheeses
Home Farm
Newton St Cyres
Exeter
Devon
EX5 5AY
Tel: 01392 851222

The shop is open Mon–Sat 9.00–3.00. Cheeses also available by mail order.

Peter and Suzanne Redstone

Middle Rocombe Farm
Stokeinteignhead
Newton Abbot
Devon
TQ12 4QL
Tel: 01626 872291
Fax: 01626 873645

Shop:
123 Union Street
Castle Circus
Torquay
TQ1 3DW

Open all year round. Mon–Sat 10.30–5.00 and on Sun 2.00–5.00.
Tel: 01803 293996 for further information.

Mail Order
Overnight delivery of a variety of ice cream packs and

hampers to England and Wales and a large part of Scotland. Special hampers for Christmas and other seasons. Credit cards taken. For further information telephone 01626 872291.

Lord and Lady Selborne

Blackmoor Apple Shop
Blackmoor
Liss
Hampshire
Tel: 01420 473782

Specialises in apples from its own orchards, pears, plums, raspberries and strawberries. There is also a range of home made produce including pies, cakes and jams as well as fresh bread, cheese, cream and ice cream, apple juices, cider and local wine. There is a play and picnic area.

Opening times: Mon–Sat 9.00–5.00; Sun 10.00–4.00.

An apple tasting Sunday is usually held at the beginning of October.

Captain Bill Swinley

Flaxley
near Newnham-on-Severn
Gloucestershire

Readers in Gloucestershire and South Wales should watch the local press in July/August for Bill's advertisements stating that his plums are ready for picking.

Julian and Diana Temperley

The Somerset Cider Brandy Co
Pass Vale Farm
Burrow Hill
Kingsbury
Martock
Somerset
TA12 5BU
Tel: 01460 240782

The Farm is open for sales of cider and cider brandy every day 11.00–5.00 except Sunday.

The Temperleys' cider may be found in many small retailers in Somerset: their cider brandy is stocked by Fortnum and Mason and by the Waitrose supermarket chain. Products are also available by mail order.

Smoked eel is available from Michael Brown on the telephone and fax numbers below.

Brown and Forrest Ltd
Thorney
Langport
Somerset
TA10 0DR
Tel: 01458 251520
Fax: 01458 253475

Hillary and Michael Thompson

Oakbank House
Blairgowrie
Perthshire
PE10 6TB
Tel: 01250 873204

For advice on growing soft fruit in Scotland contact Michael Thompson.

Mike and Julie Turner

The Big Sheep
Bideford
Devon
EX39 5AP
Tel: 01237 472366

Opening hours are broadly 10.00–6.00 all year round. Entrance is free during the winter when there are fewer activities available, but it is worth telephoning ahead in the winter months to check on opening arrangements.

Guy and Sheila Woodall

Thorncroft Limited
Manor Farm
Alresford
Hampshire
SO24 9DH

Tel: 01962 736200
Fax: 01962 734025

Thorncroft do not supply by mail order but their products may be found in major supermarkets (e.g. Sainsbury's, Safeway), Holland and Barratt and independent health food

Index